Goderich Ontario in Photos, Saving Our History One Photo at a Time

Photography
by Barbara Raué
2012

Series Name:
Cruising Ontario

Book 23: Goderich

Cover photo: 85 Essex Street

Series Name: Cruising Ontario

Book 1: London
Book 2: Dundas
Book 3: Hamilton
Book 4: Oakville
Book 5: Chesley
Book 6: Stoney Creek
Book 7: Waterdown
Book 8: Owen Sound
Book 9: Mount Forest
Book 10: Dundalk
Book 11: Burford and Area
Book 12: Waterford and Area
Book 13: Drumbo and Area
Book 14: Sheffield and Area
Book 15: Tavistock and Area
Book 16: Ancaster and Mount Hope
Book 17: Innerkip
Book 18: Brantford
Book 19: Burlington
Book 20: Guelph and Area
Book 21: Ayr
Book 22: Erin
Book 23: Goderich

Other Books by Barbara Raue

Coins of Gold

Arrows, Indians and Love

The Life and Times of Barbara
Volume 1: Inventions That Have Enhanced My Life
Volume 2: Entertainment That I Have Enjoyed
Volume 3: East Coast Trips
Volume 4: Olympics
Volume 5: Wonders of the World
Volume 6: Caribbean Cruises
Volume 7: Animals
Volume 8: Storms
Volume 9: Wars

Goderich

Goderich is located on the eastern shore of Lake Huron. The town was laid out in 1828. The downtown has an octagonal traffic circle known as "The Square." Ringed by eight commercial blocks, The Square reflects a vision of a town centre of classical design and elegance. From the 1840s to the 1890s, the growth of Goderich centered around the development of the Market Square. For nearly 100 years the original Huron County Courthouse, an Italianate brick building of imposing scale and elegance, stood in the centre of The Square. The current courthouse replaced the original which was destroyed by fire in 1954. This fast growing town was the centre of a prosperous agricultural region. The Sifto Salt Mines are located under Lake Huron.

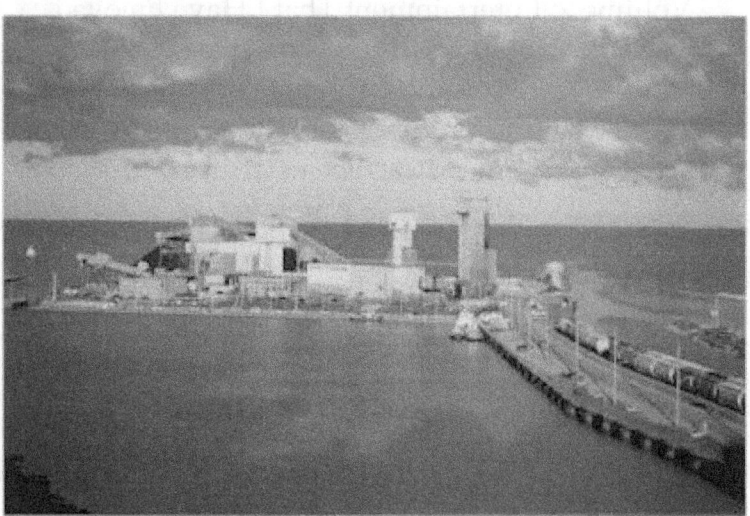

Salt Mining in Huron County – 1876

On May 17, 1866 while drilling for oil near Goderich, Ontario, Samuel Platt and Peter MacEwan instead struck salt at 965 feet. Within a year, the pioneer well at Goderich was able to declare a profit of 31%. Such success naturally led to competition and numerous blocks soon sprung up as the salt bonanza spread. By 1872, twelve Goderich companies were producing 2,000 barrels of salt per day. The manufacture of salt quickly extended inland as good quality brine was also discovered at Clinton and Seaforth. The large quantities of wood required in the brine evaporation process quickly depleted forests in the immediate vicinity of Goderich. As fuel became more expensive, the competitive advantage shifted towards the inland salt makers. Located along the Grand Trunk Railway, Clinton and Seaforth easily captured the domestic market to the East. Goderich was left to the export trade, shipping salt to American markets in Milwaukee and Chicago.

After putting down salt wells in Dublin, Brusssels and Seaforth, Peter MacEwan returned to Goderich where he established the International Salt Company.

During the "boom" years of the 1870s, the majority of salt production resulted from the evaporation of brine.

In 1956 the Sifto Salt Company began exploratory work. A shaft was sunk to a depth of 1,760 feet and salt production began near the end of 1959. Initially intended to extract 500,000 tons per year, the mine was expanded and by 1983 had a capacity of 3,600,000 tons. Seventy percent of the salt is shipped by vessel to Canadian and U.S. markets along the Great Lakes system.

Upon hearing of the Goderich find, Henry Ramsford instructed his son Richard to put down a well on their property near Clinton, Ontario. At its height during the 1870s the Stapleton Salt Works employed over 100 men. Stapleton boasted an evaporation plant, a cooperage and sawmill, as well as cottages for the workers. Turning out 300 barrels of salt a day, the Stapleton works carried on for 50 years until 1918.

Fred W. Doty established the Doty Engine Company Limited in 1905 on the corner of Brock and Victoria Streets in Goderich. At its peak, the Doty Engine Company employed over 80 workers and made marine steam engines for use on the Great Lakes. During the Great War the Doty Engine Company produced artillery shells and engines for British and American warships. The company was sold to W. H. Hutchins in 1917 and renamed the National Shipbuilding Co. Ltd.

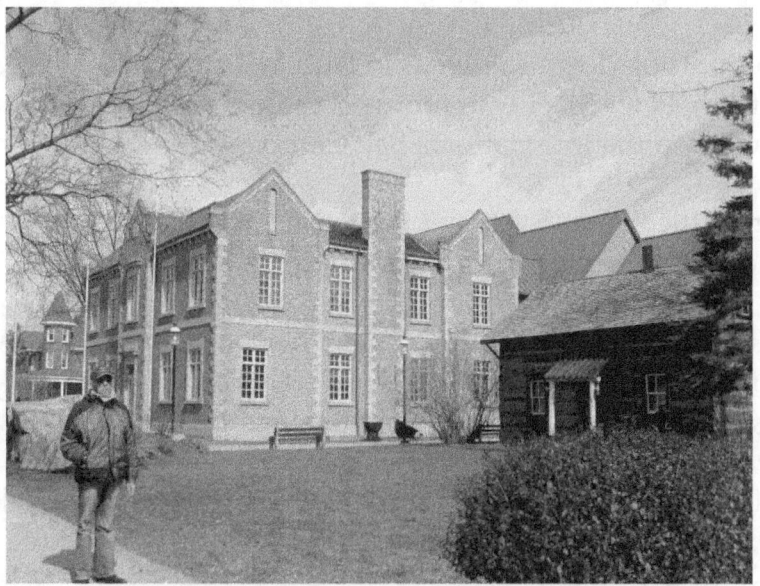

Huron County Museum, 110 North Street

The Huron County Museum

The oldest part of the museum structure, was once Goderich's major public school. Known as "Central School", the attractive building was built in 1856 and served the town's elementary students for almost 100 years. During the period 1876-1910, it also housed the Goderich Model School for teaching future teachers. Because of an expanding population, a second large school (Victoria Public School) was built in 1910 at the south end of town. Central School continued to serve the students from the north side of Goderich until 1950. By that time Victoria School had been upgraded and expanded to hold the entire public school population and Central School was closed.

The Central School building was obtained from the school board by the County of Huron in 1950 to house the large collection of antiques and artefacts which became the Huron County Museum.

The school, described as being of the Elizabethan or Tudor-Gothic tradition, was designed by William Thomas, one of nineteenth-century Canada's most sought-after architects. (Thomas has 30 churches to his credit as well as other notable structures such as the St. Lawrence Centre in Toronto and the Brock Monument at Queenston.). The school was constructed from local brick by Goderich master-builder, Thomas Kneeshaw.

The original Museum collection was brought together by Mr. Joseph Herbert Neill as a result of a lifetime of collecting. In 1948, he sold all of his 4,000 objects to the County of Huron for an average price of one dollar per object and with two conditions. First, that the County establish a public museum and second, that he be made the Curator for as long as he wished to hold the position.

Huron County Museum opened in June 1950. Over the next fifteen years, Mr. Neill worked to complete exhibits and add buildings to the site of the Museum and by the time he retired in 1965 the Museum had grown to over 42,000 square feet filled to the rafters with artefacts from all over the County.

Mr. Neill's Log Cabin, which is located on the front lawn of the Huron County Museum, was built in 1875 near Bluevale, a Huron County community. It was moved to its current site in 1953 and was used by Mr. Neill until 1965, when he had to be moved to Huronview, a home for the aged, because of his failing health; he passed away in 1969. The log cabin is home to the Goderich branch of the Ontario Genealogical Society.

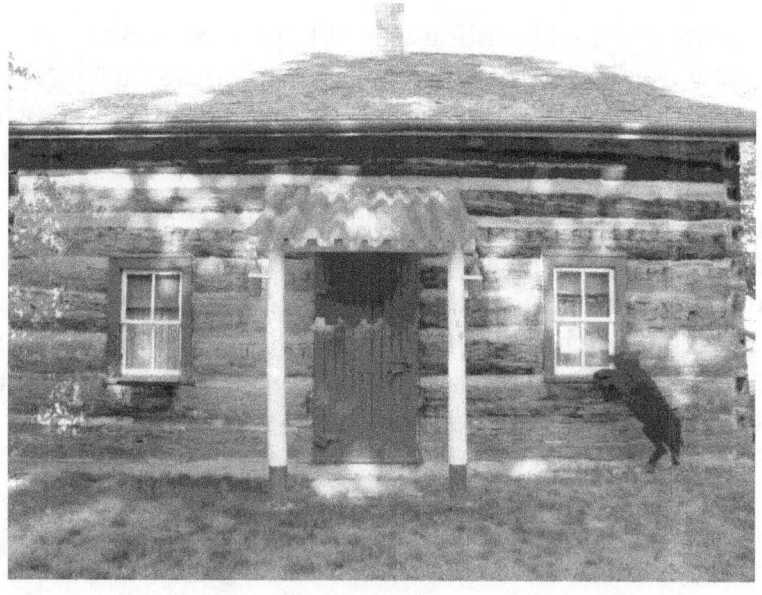

In 1989, a new addition for the museum was opened that replaced all but the Central School building.

When the pioneers first arrived at their homestead, they had to clear the land. The trees that were cut down were used to build the settlers first homes. First, the settlers built a foundation for their log cabin to sit on, usually with dry stone using no mortar to hold the stone together. The foundation kept the logs from touching the ground, protecting them from rotting. Next logs were cut into the appropriate size for their cabin and all branches and bark were removed. The remnants from the logs were used for firewood. The logs were notched at the ends so they could be locked together to create a secure structure. Two notched logs were laid down on two parallel, opposite ends of the foundation. A third log was placed so that the notches fit together at a right angle. These steps were repeated until the walls were finished. The roof could be made with the use of hollowed half-logs. A row of these logs would be placed hollow side up, while a second row would be placed hollow side down. One log would be placed in the center of the two logs beneath it. This construction allowed the rain to drain off the roof without dripping into the cabin. Another way to construct the roof was to gradually shorten the logs of two walls to create a point, a gable. The roof could then be constructed out of logs of a smaller diameter and covered with shingles. The doors and windows were cut out of the walls and a fireplace was built out of mud if there were no stones available. A heavy blanket covered the door, and animal bladder or greased paper was stretched over the windows. The final step in the construction of the log cabin was to fill all of the cracks. This was done with wood, moss, or plaster made of mud and straw. This helped protect the family from the wind. The floor of the cabin was made of the compressed soil, or of planks that were cut from logs. Many log cabins were one room structures of about 10 feet x 12 feet. This was used as both a kitchen, and a place to sleep. Some peaked roof log cabins would have a sleeping loft above the main room.

When the first settlers arrived in Huron County, there were no supermarkets or grocery stores, so they had to provide food for themselves. They hunted and trapped animals, caught fish in the rivers and lakes, and gathered herbs, roots, and berries from the woods. The rest of their food was provided by their fields, gardens and farmyards. Along with fruits and vegetables, the settlers raised pigs, cows, chickens, ducks, and goats. During the spring and summer, maple syrup, honey, eggs, and fresh vegetables that were grown in the garden were a large part of their diet. During the fall and winter, venison, wild geese, hares, chicken, turkey, and dried apples were their primary source of food. Root vegetables, such as carrots, potatoes and onions were stored so that they were able to be eaten year round. Salt pork, cornmeal, oatmeal, bread, milk, cheese and butter were also on hand for consumption year round.

Cooking was done over a fireplace or on a wood stove. The heat of the fire depended on the type and amount of wood used. The fire had to be watched carefully to maintain a steady and consistent heat for baking in the oven. The hardships of the early pioneers ensured that they never wasted food and all leftovers were put to good use. Pancakes were a staple in pioneer families and were often fried to feed a gathering of farm workers.

Farming in Huron County

When the first settlers came to what is now Huron County, their first priority was to clear a plot of land to build their first permanent dwelling. After the settlers had cleared a few acres of land and planted their crops, they established a permanent dwelling and barn. By the mid 19th century, Huron County was an active agricultural center in Ontario. Agriculture became more mechanized with the introduction of various farm implements and machinery, including the threshing machine and steam engine. Today, Huron County continues to be very agriculturally productive. Many descendants of the original 19th century settlers still live and farm in Huron County.

After the harvest, the grain was ready to be threshed, the process of removing the seed or grain from the stalk of a harvested crop. The earliest known method of threshing was to beat the grain from the stalk with a stick.

Later a flail was used to separate the grain. A flail is made of two or more wooden sticks or poles that are held together with a piece of chain or leather. One stick is held, while the other strikes a pile of grain, loosening the husks. The flail was most likely developed in Europe during the Middle Ages and continued to be used until the late 19th century. Threshing with a flail was usually done in a barn on a specially prepared "threshing floor", which had wide open doors at either end. Using a flail about 5 to 6 bushels of grain could be threshed per day. The open doors allowed for a constant flow of air which separated the chaff from the grain. This is called winnowing and is a very time consuming process. On a windy day, the chaff and grain were tossed into the air. The lighter chaff blew away, leaving the heavier grain to fall to the ground or barn floor.

The Fanning Mill was invented to separate the chaff from the grain. By turning the crank, the fan caused the air to blow around the screens. As the chaff and grain traveled from a hopper above, the fan flew the lighter chaff free, leaving the heavier grain to fall through the screens.

The first practical threshing machine was invented by Andrew Miekle, a Scottish mechanical engineer, in 1786. It combined the threshing and winnowing processes into one machine greatly speeding up the threshing process.

Large farm owners usually owned their own threshing machine, but many smaller farm owners relied on custom "threshermen" to do the threshing work for them.

 The Steam Traction Engine was introduced in the 1880s but didn't replace the treadmill powered thresher until the 1890s. This raised the amount that could be threshed to about 1,000 bushels per day. The Steam Thresher was operated by large crews of men who went from farm to farm threshing grain for 3 or 4 months in the fall. The *Threshermen's Waterwagon* was introduced around 1900. Every steam powered thresher came with a water wagon to supply the steam engine with water. It was usually pulled by two horses. The average thresher needed four to six tanks of water per day. The water was pumped from cisterns, water troughs or ponds in the vicinity by the water boy.

The Combine Harvester combines the harvesting and threshing processes. The development of the combine began with Samuel Lane's invention which was patented in 1828. It had a reaping and threshing mechanism, a winnowing fan and a sack filling mechanism. The early combines were drawn by horse. Eventually steam or gasoline powered tractors were used to pull the combine. The self-powered combine was first introduced in 1928 and developed into the combine as we know it today.

The most commonly grown crops in Huron County include corn, white beans, soy beans, wheat and barley.

Children of the Victorian era did not have the status and rights of today's youth. Class dictated lifestyle. Children of the upper classes were relegated to the nursery in separate quarters of the home and raised by a nanny. Middle class youngsters had their own domestic chores and responsibilities. Poorer children were forced into hard labour in often unhealthy conditions. Many children died before the age of 5 from diseases easily treatable today.

In the early days, sending the children to school was not always easy. A group of parents had to get together to build a school, hire a teacher, as well as pay their wages, and buy the necessary school supplies. Until the school was built, school was often held in a settler's home, the general store or the village church. The first school houses were single log cabins with two or three rows of benches and tables.

In a pioneer household, everyone had many chores to do. Young boys were responsible for feeding the livestock and gathering firewood. Older boys and men were in charge of making furniture, building fences, cutting down trees for lumber, clearing the field, shearing sheep, plowing, planting and harvesting crops, digging wells, slaughtering livestock and much more. Young girls' chores included feeding the chickens and gathering eggs, spinning wool, making clothing and blankets, milking the cows, making butter and cheese among other things.

Attitudes toward children changed in the late 19th century. Parents began to realize that children needed to play instead of working all the time. Elementary Education became tuition-free in 1871 with the Common School Act: the law stipulated that children between the ages of 7 and 12 must attend school for at least 4 months per year. Principles of imperialism, capitalism and Christianity formed the Canadianization of school programs.

Keeping Warm in Huron County

The Europeans who came to settle in Huron County during the 1800s were often unprepared for the harsh winters that awaited them.

The rigorous Canadian winter demanded more than the traditional fireplace which had sufficed in England and France. The cast iron stove offered a useful remedy for the inadequacies of the fireplace.

However, the stove was far from the ideal means of heating a building. It produced extreme variation in temperature within a room, and usually created the discomfort of draughts, and created a foul atmosphere. With the building of bigger and better stoves, attempts were made to better regulate its heat, and to improve ventilation. In keeping with Victorian tastes, manufacturers covered their stoves with ornate decoration. Classical Greek and Gothic designs were featured on many of the 55,000 stoves turned out annually by twenty-eight Canadian firms.

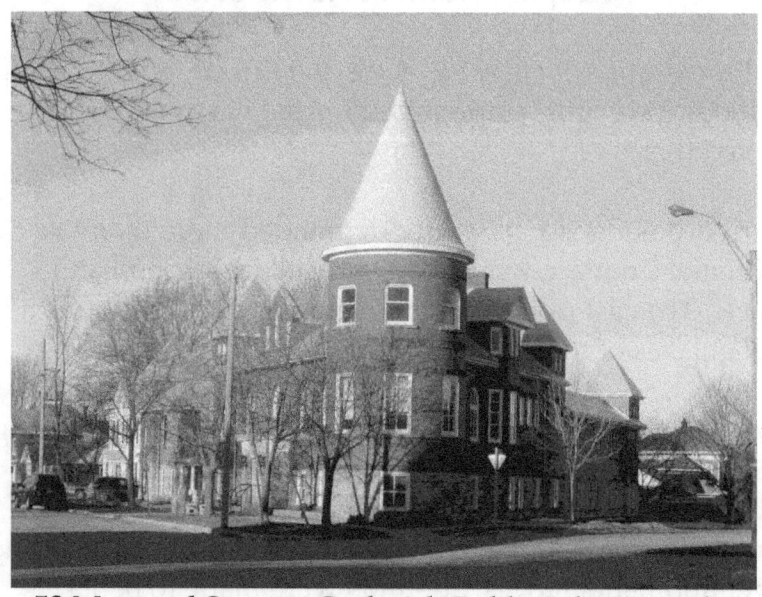

52 Montreal Street – Goderich Public Library in the Romanesque Revival style with the large round tower, the round-headed windows, and the irregular roof

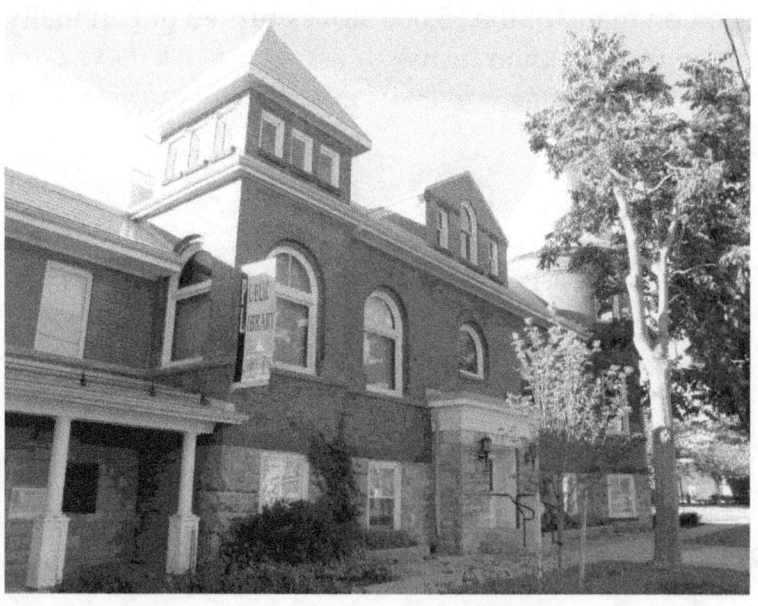

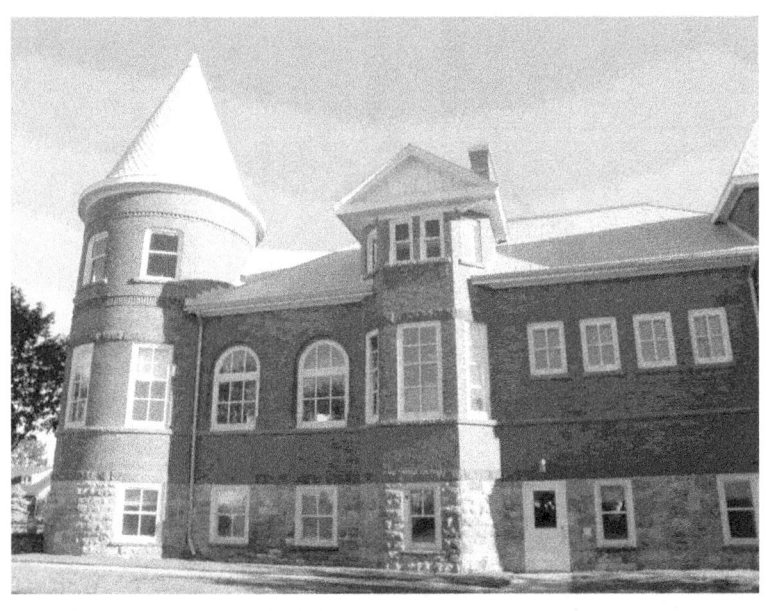

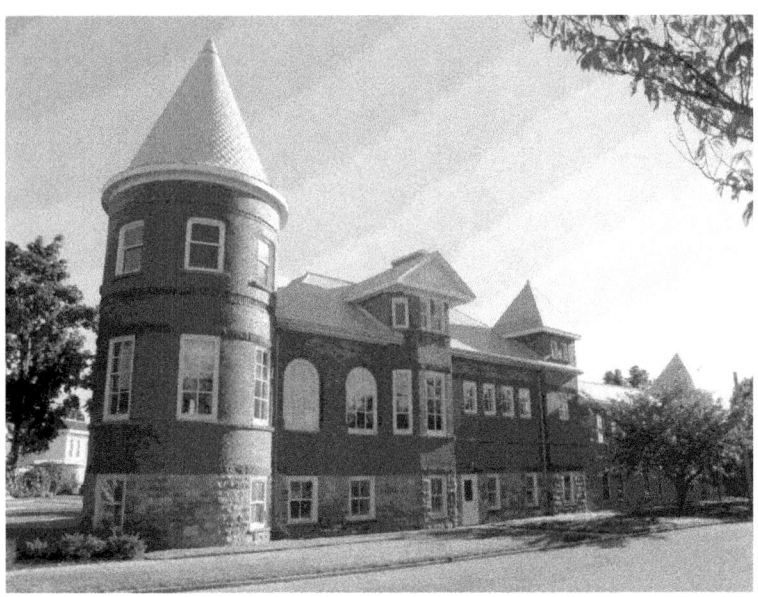

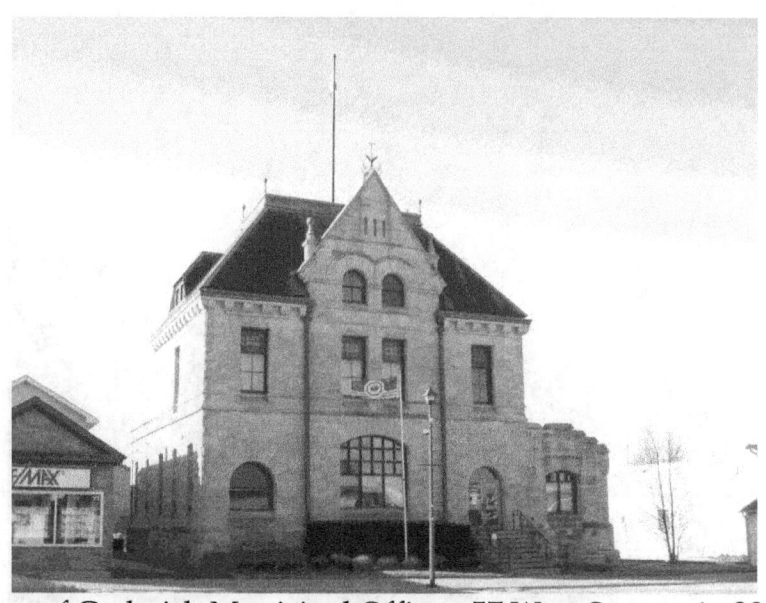

Port of Goderich Municipal Offices, 57 West Street – in 2007
Built in 1890 of stone in the Romanesque style with massive
gables

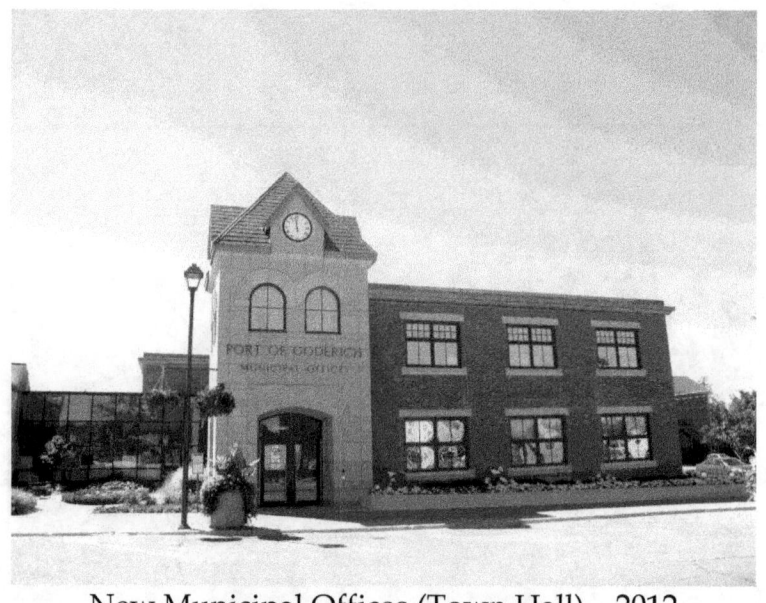

New Municipal Offices (Town Hall) – 2012

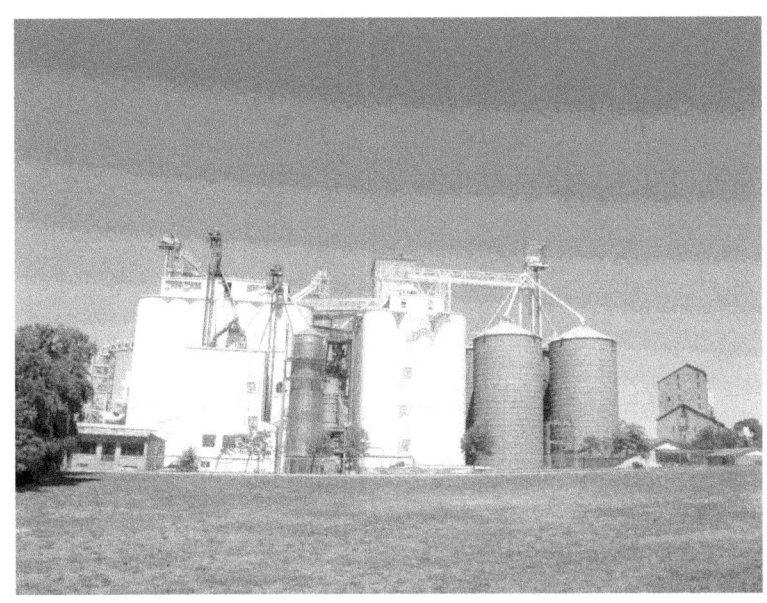

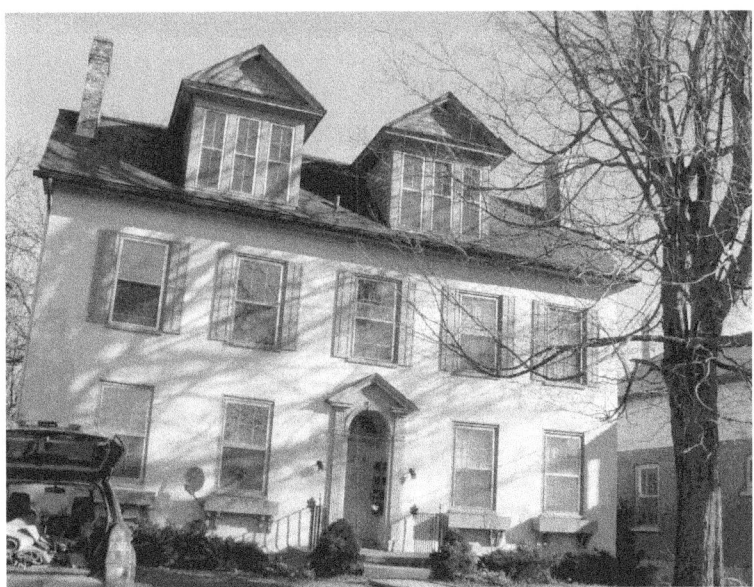

116 West Street - Neo-classical style characterized by its rectangular shape, low-pitched roof, an elaborate entranceway and large dormer windows

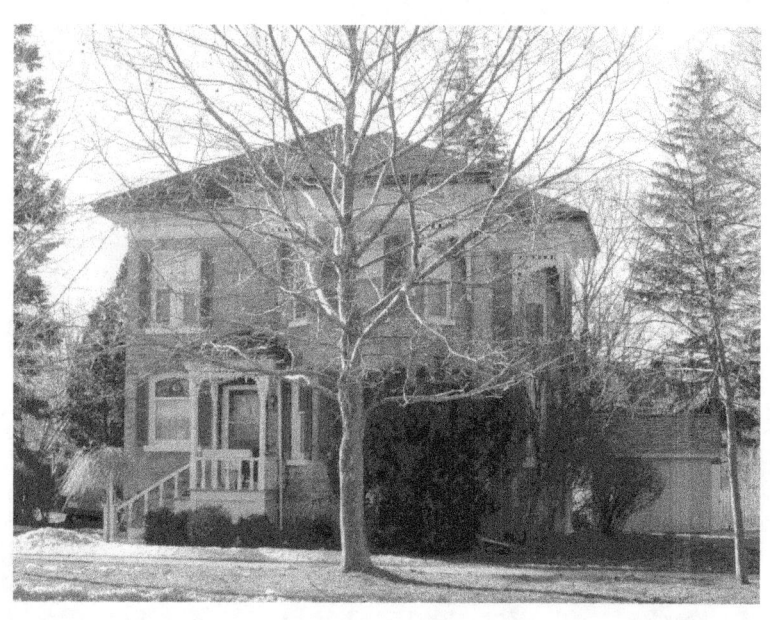

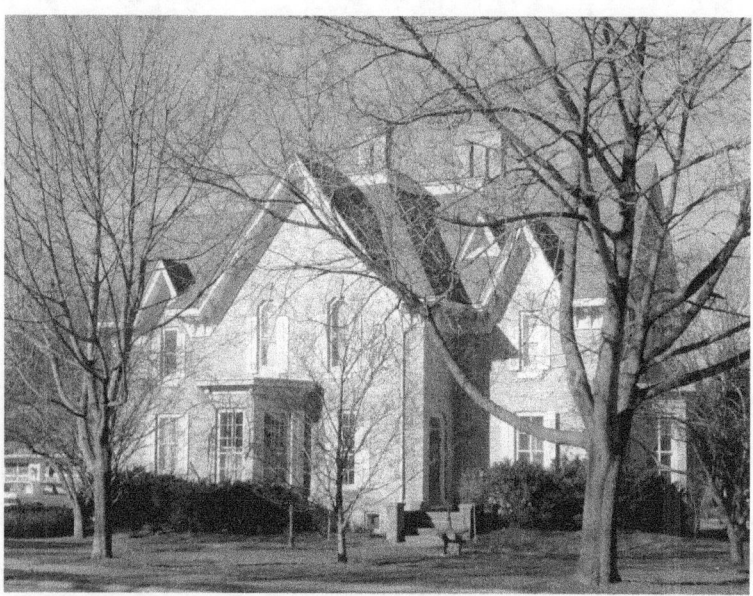

Gothic style

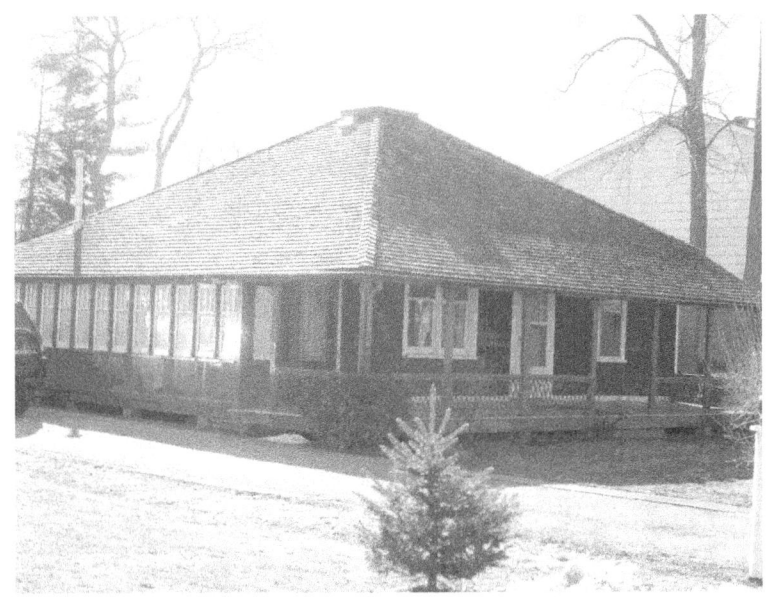

135 Essex Street c. 1880
lakefront cottage in the Picturesque style

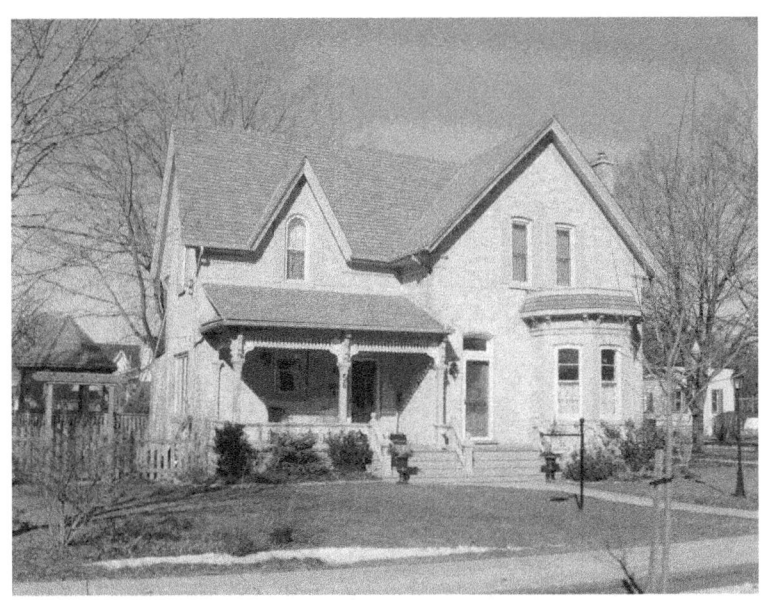

56 Wellesley Street

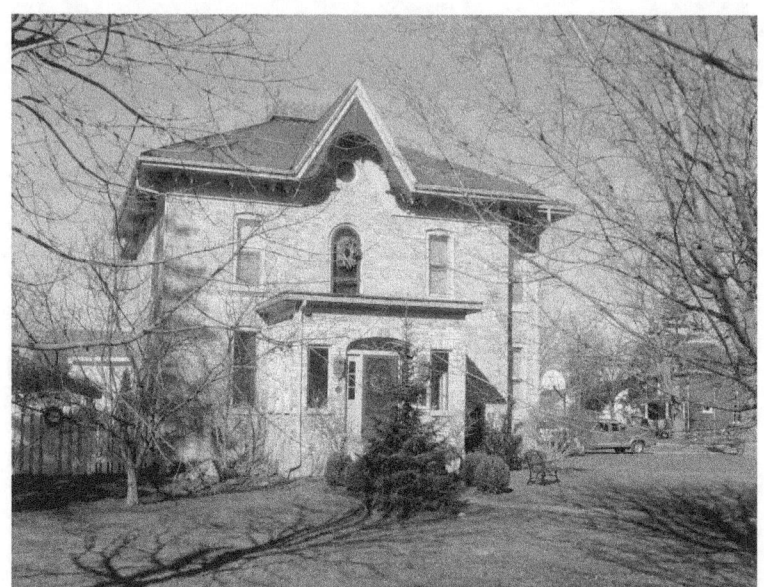

82 Wellesley Street - erected in 1888, this house is notable for iron cresting on the roof peak, decorative brackets and fascia boards under the soffits, decorative fretwork around the centre gable, metal roofing tiles, and the square bay on the west side. The house is an example of the large Georgian structures built throughout Ontario in the latter part of the 19th century.

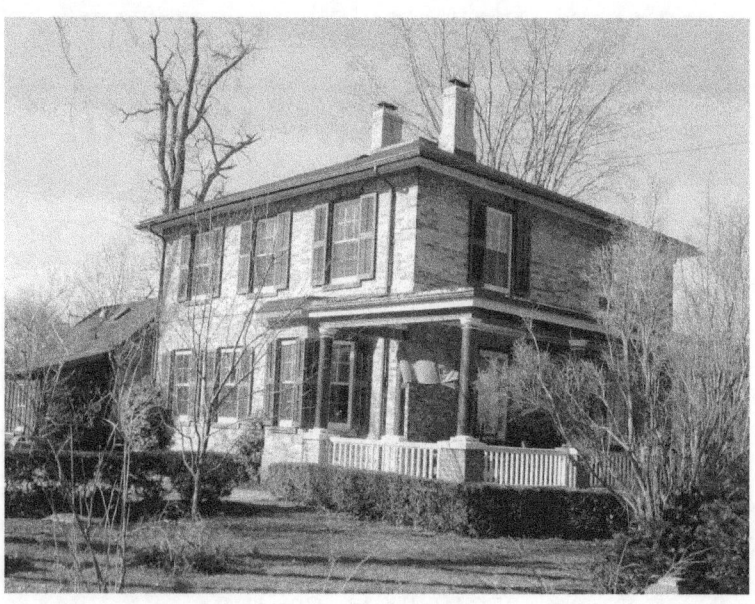

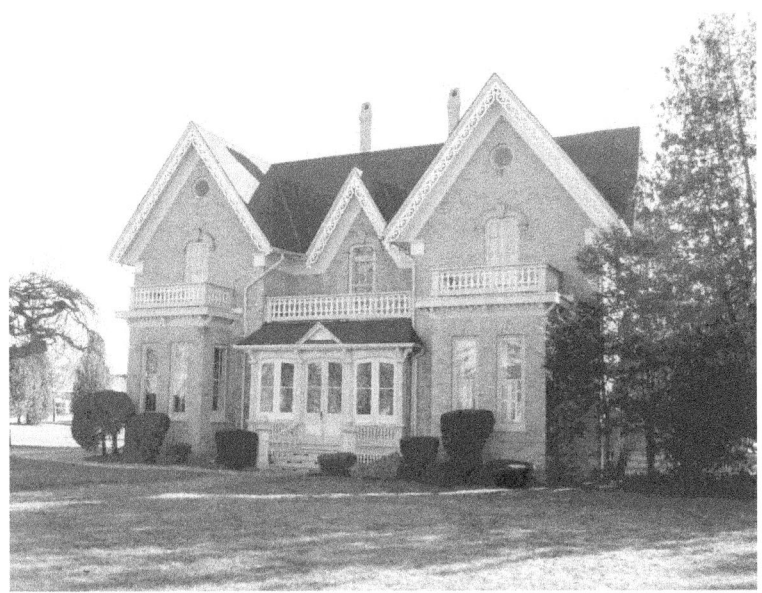

85 Essex Street – "The Judges House" is a white brick High Victorian structure with a Gothic Revival flavour with Tudor Revival or Italianate features. It derives its elegance from the symmetry of the three-bay façade. The symmetry is further emphasized by the square bay windows on the first floor as well as the central porch under the central dormer. The delicacy of the wooden bargeboards and rails over the bay windows add pleasing touches.

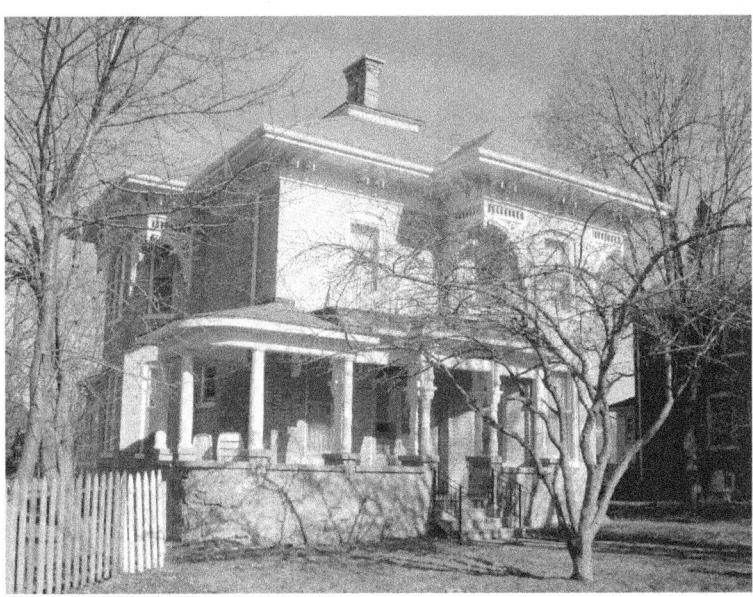

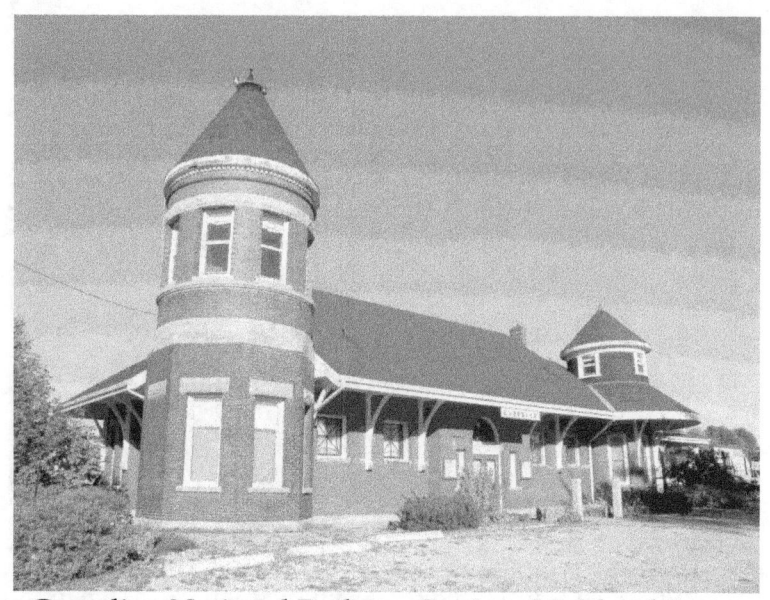

Canadian National Railway Station, Maitland Street
built in 1902 of red brick

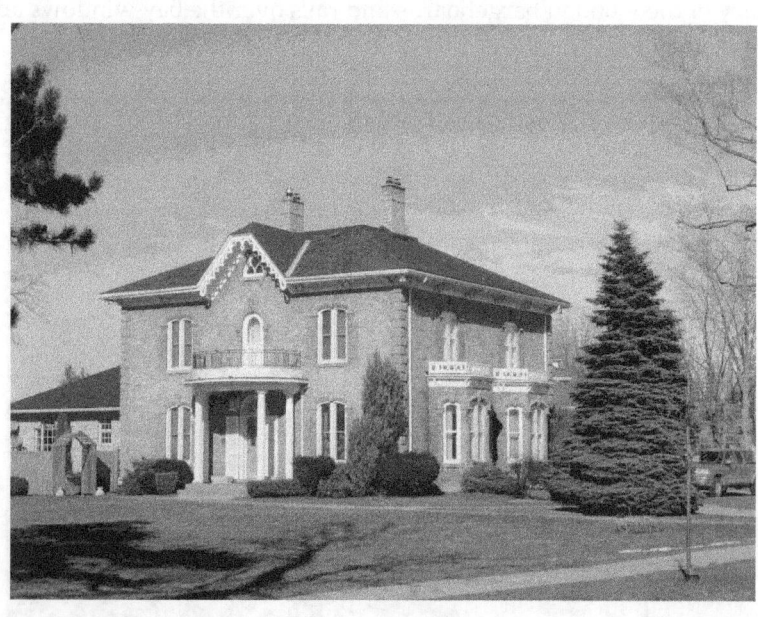

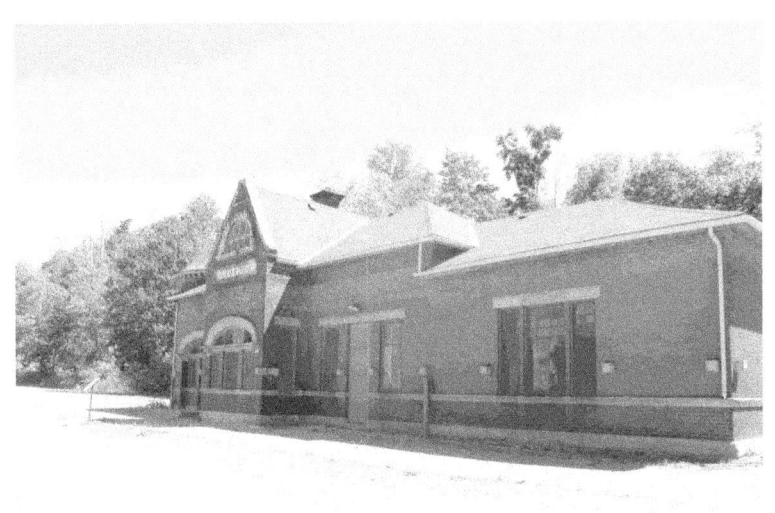

Canadian Pacific Railway station

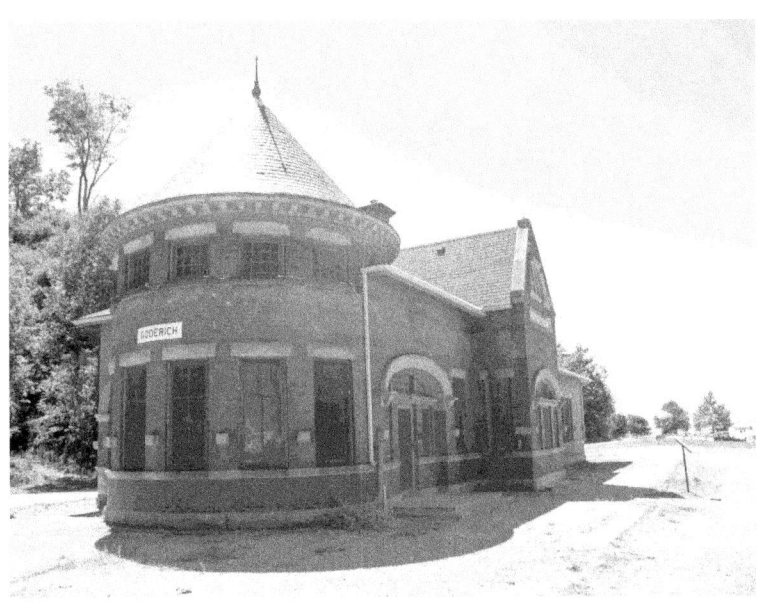

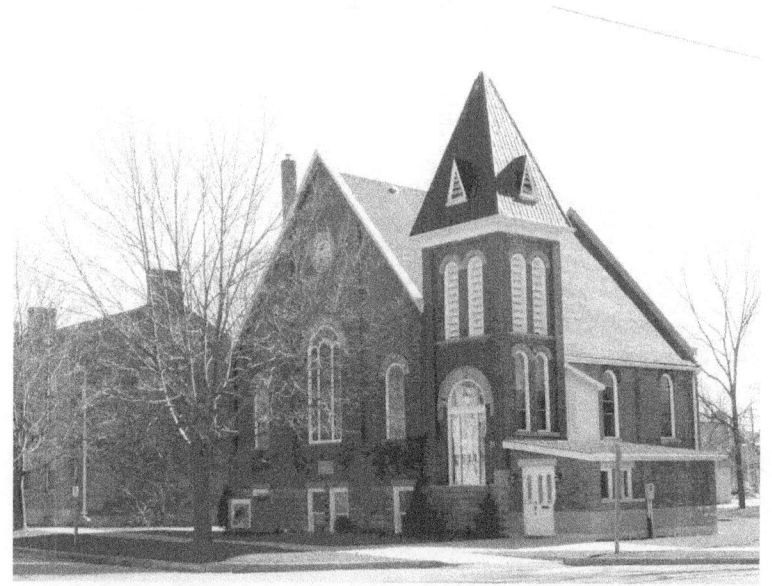

First Baptist Church on corner of Market Street - A.D. 1906

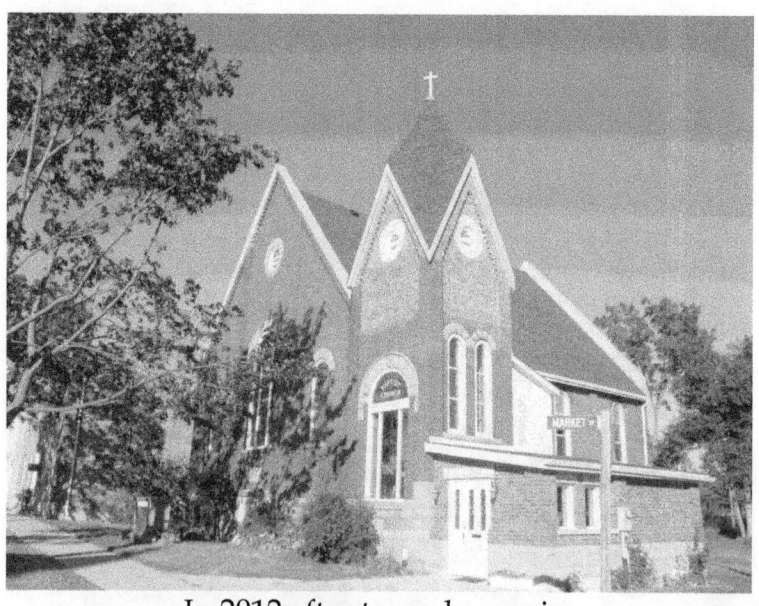

In 2012 after tornado repairs

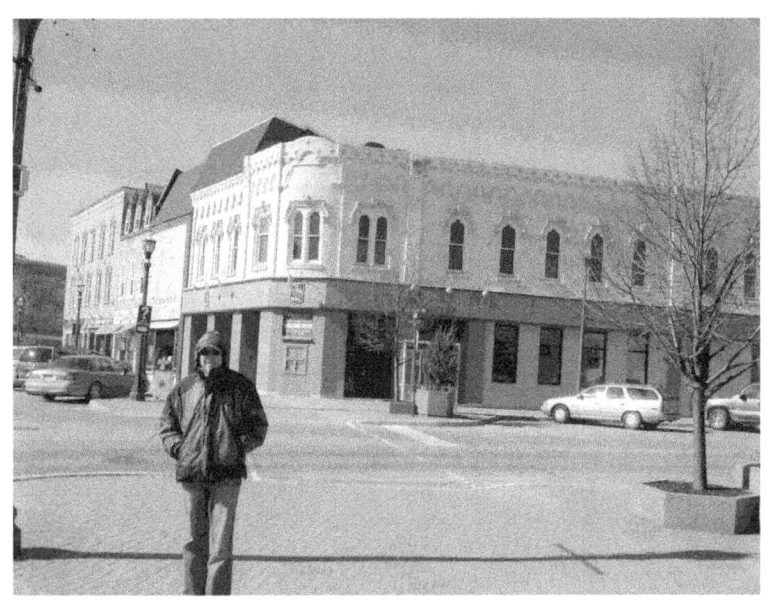

Downtown Square

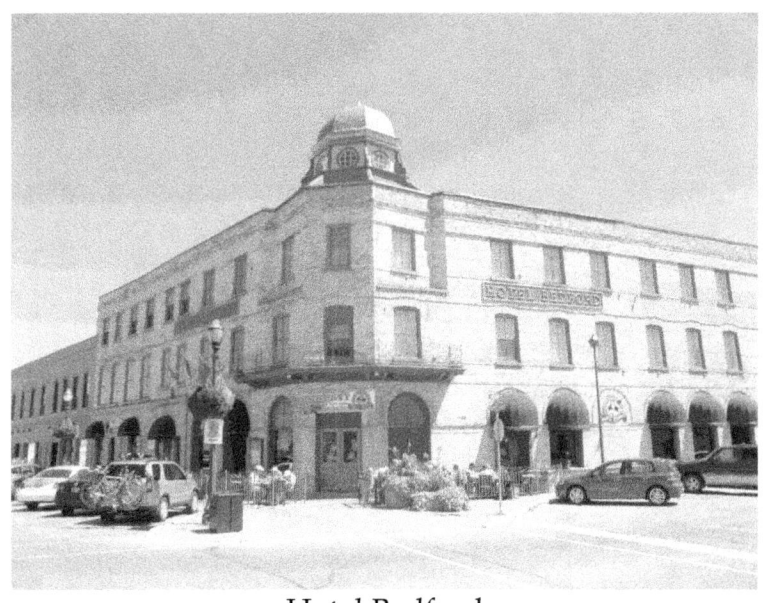

Hotel Bedford

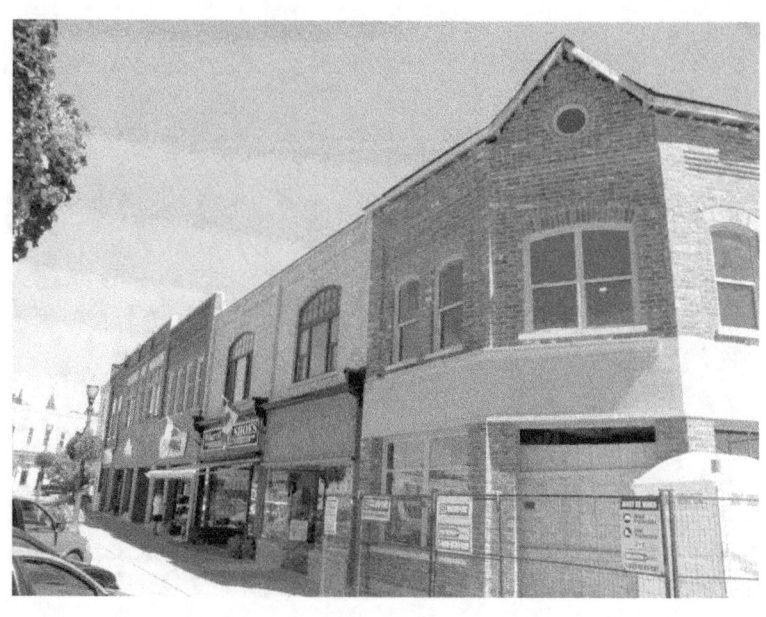

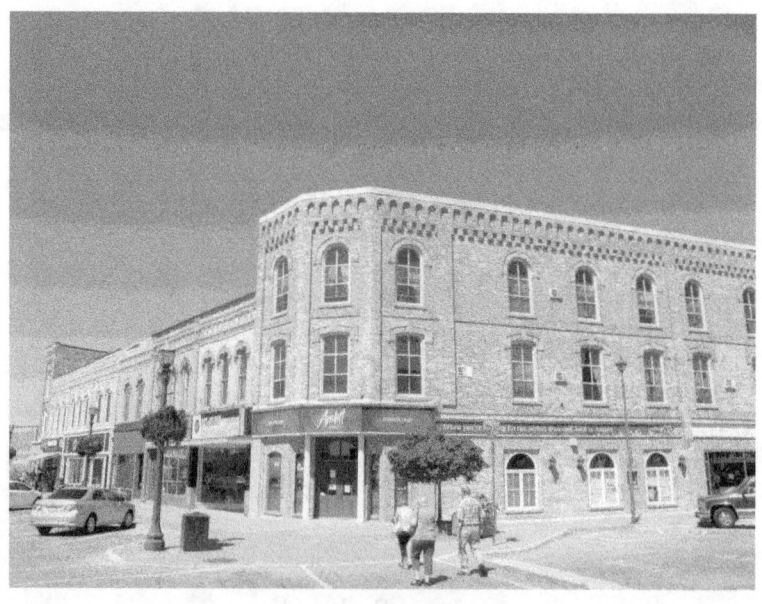

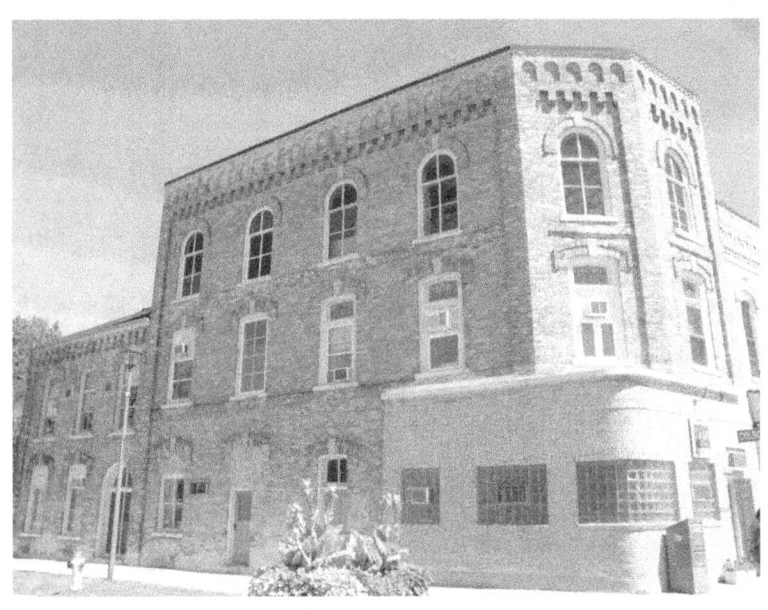

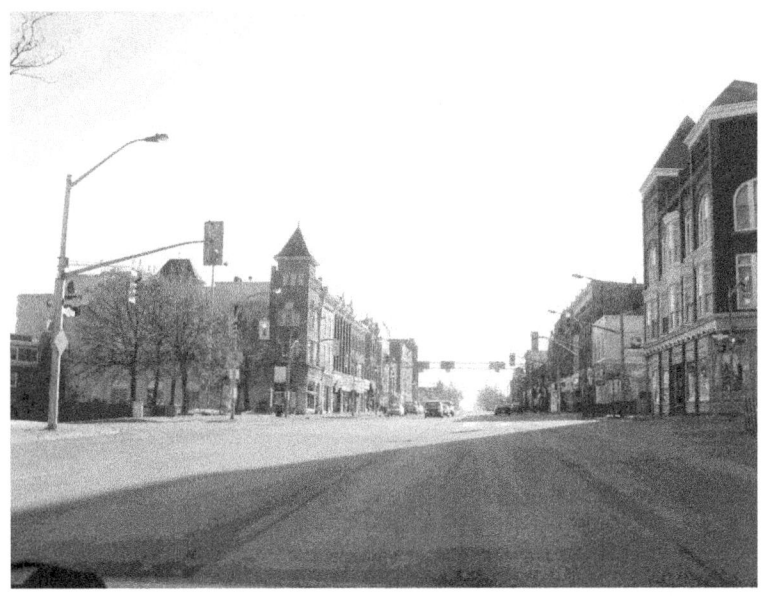

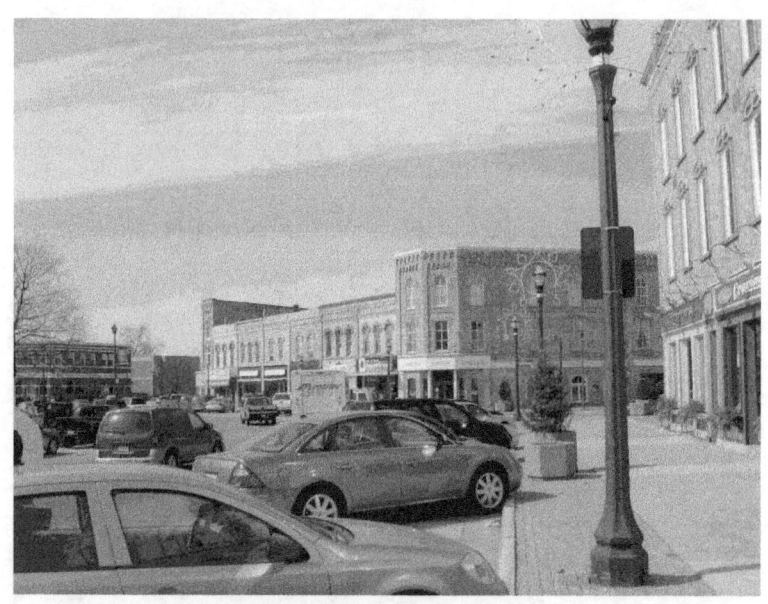

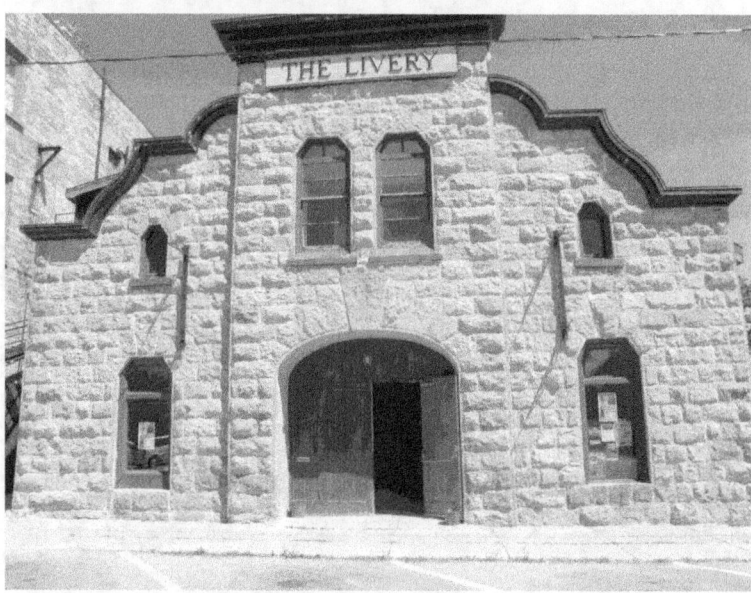

The Livery, 5 South Street – 1878 made of cut stone
Shaped gable, parapet, unusual windows

Huron County Court House

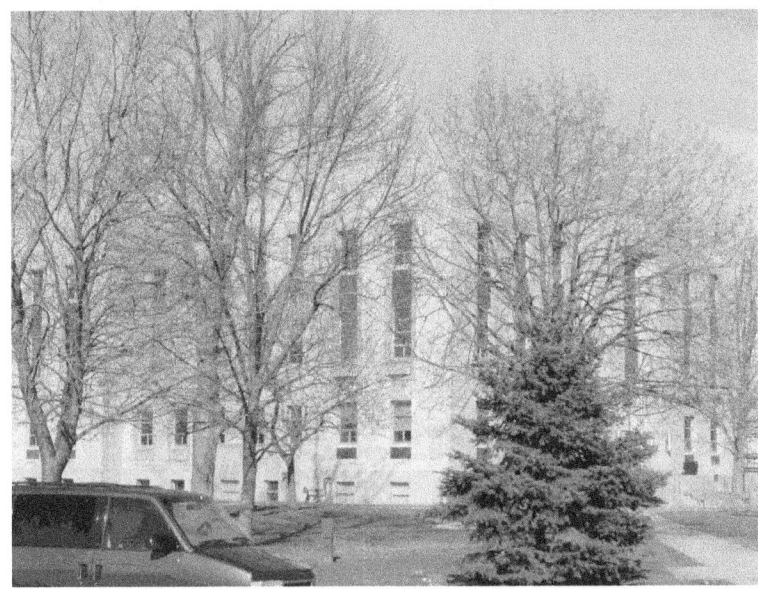

In 2007 with lots of trees before the tornado

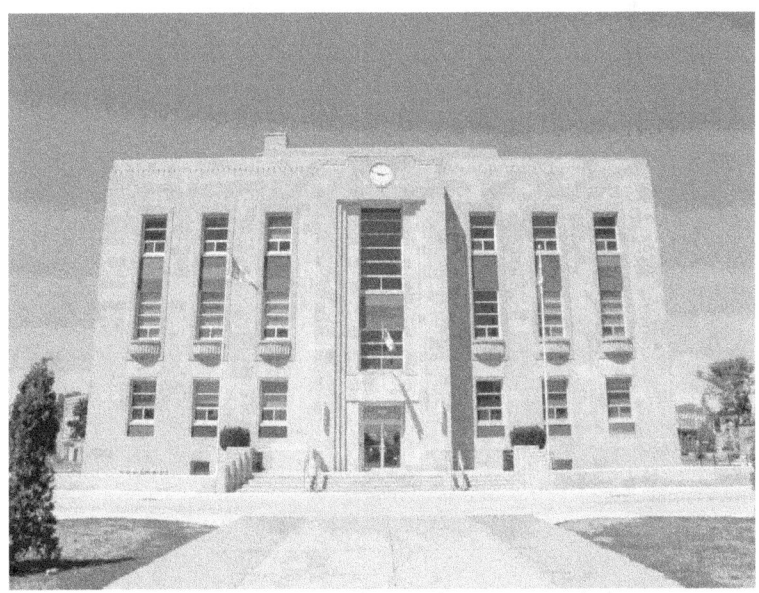

After the tornado with no trees left

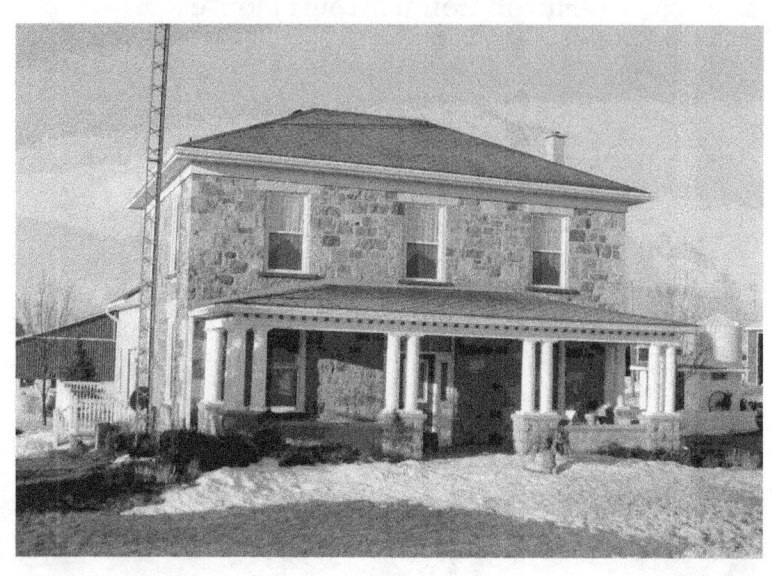

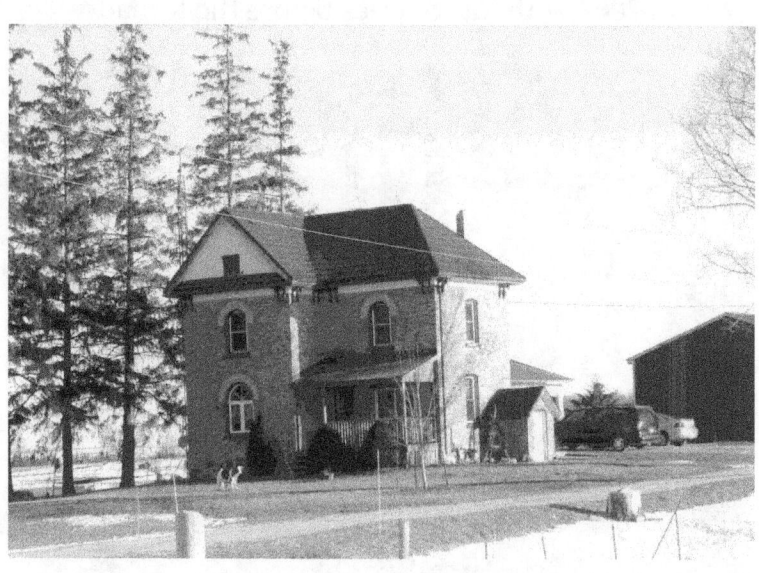

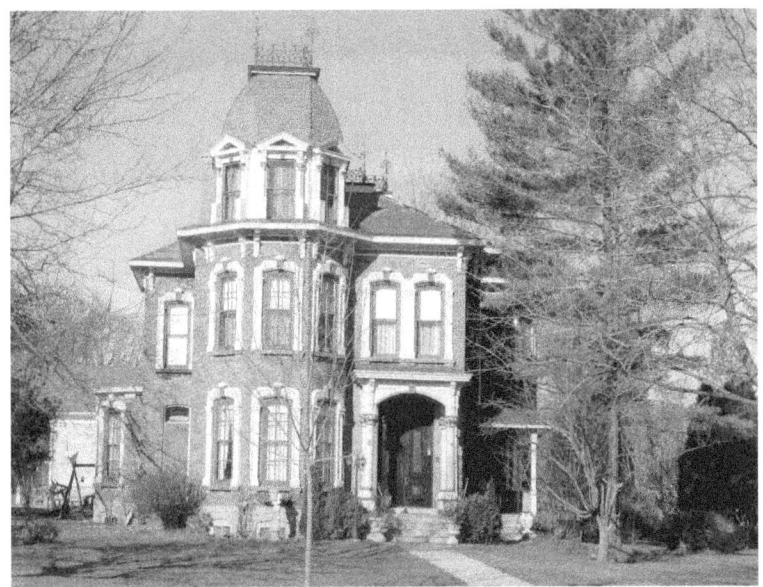

20 Wellington Street South - The "Strachan House" features include the mansard-roofed corner tower, the heavily modeled window headings, the patterned shingles, and the iron cresting crowning the roof.

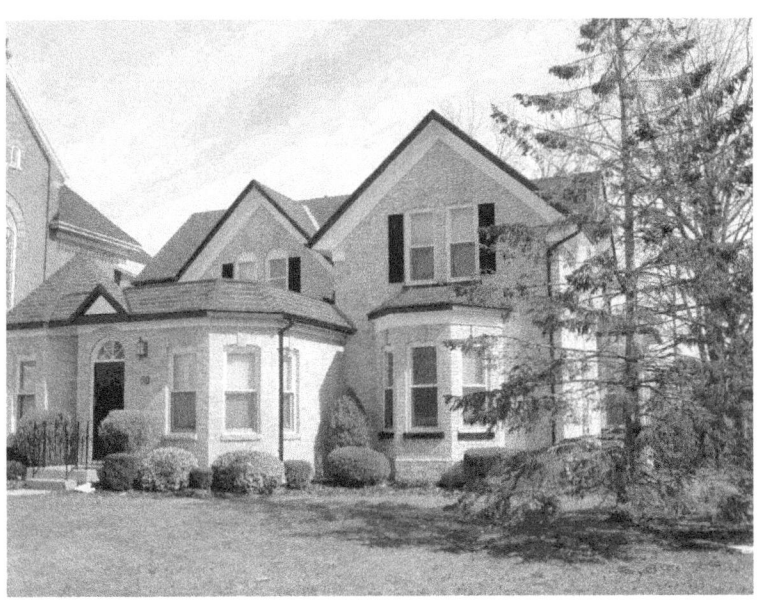

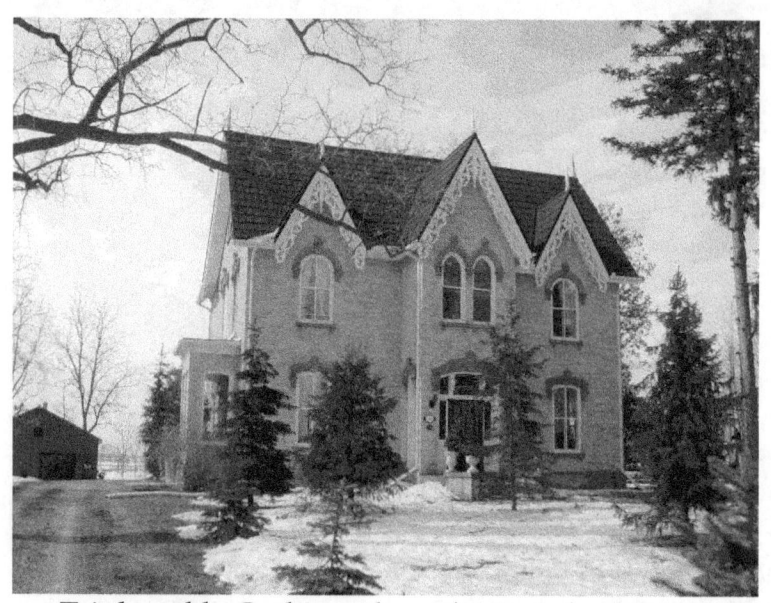

Triple-gable Gothic style with gingerbread trim

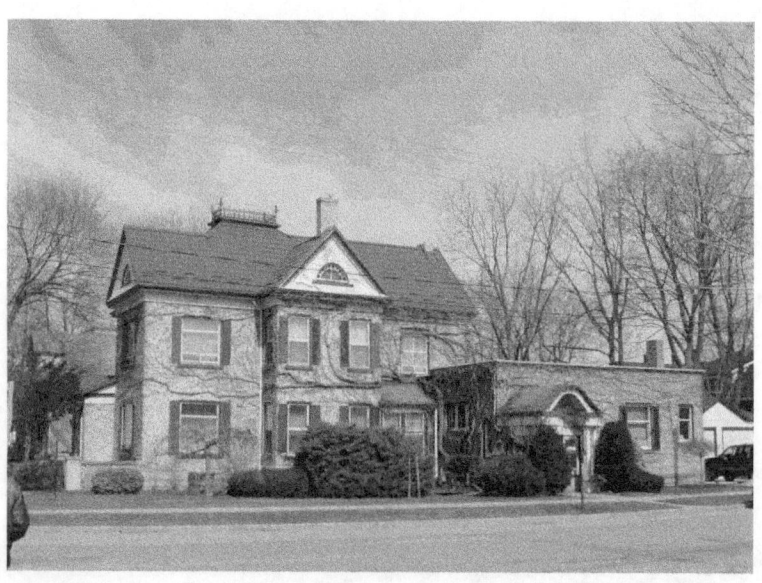

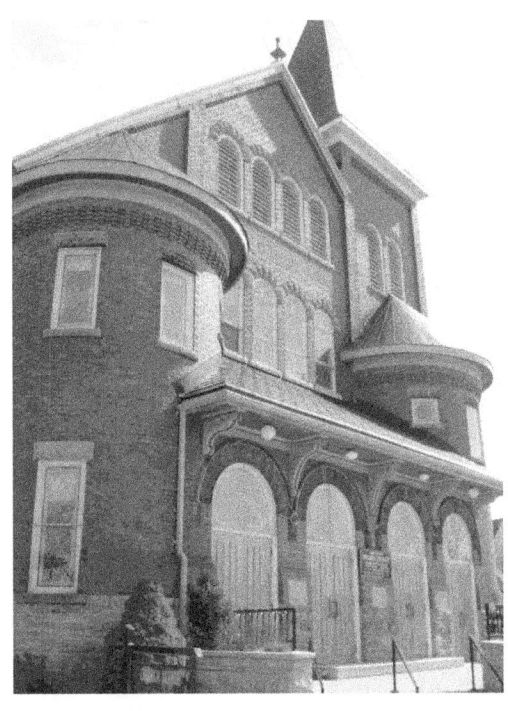

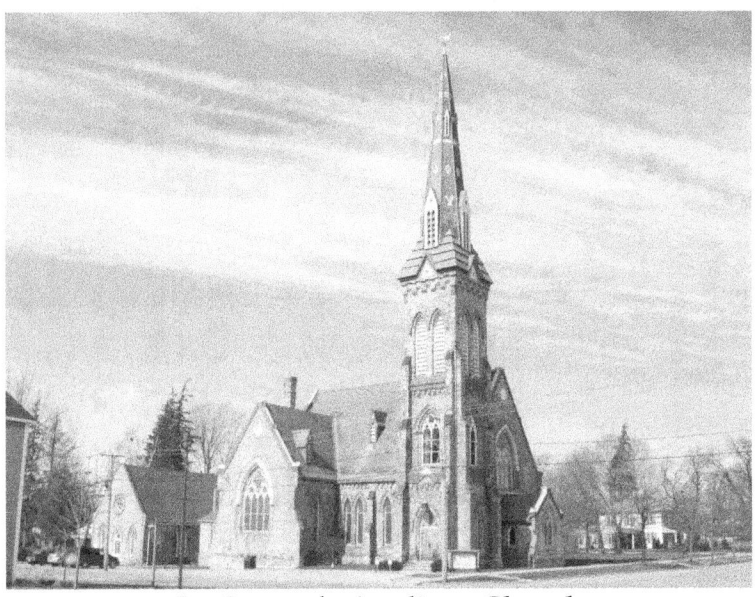

St. George's Anglican Church

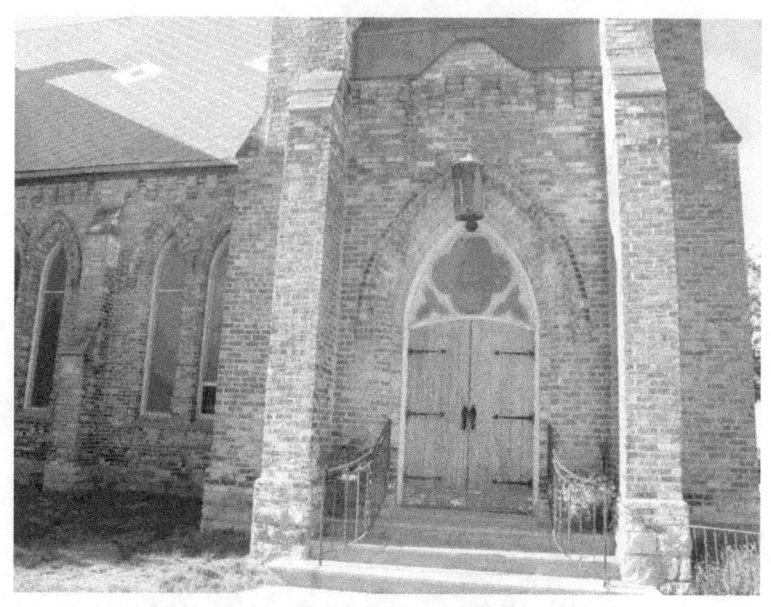

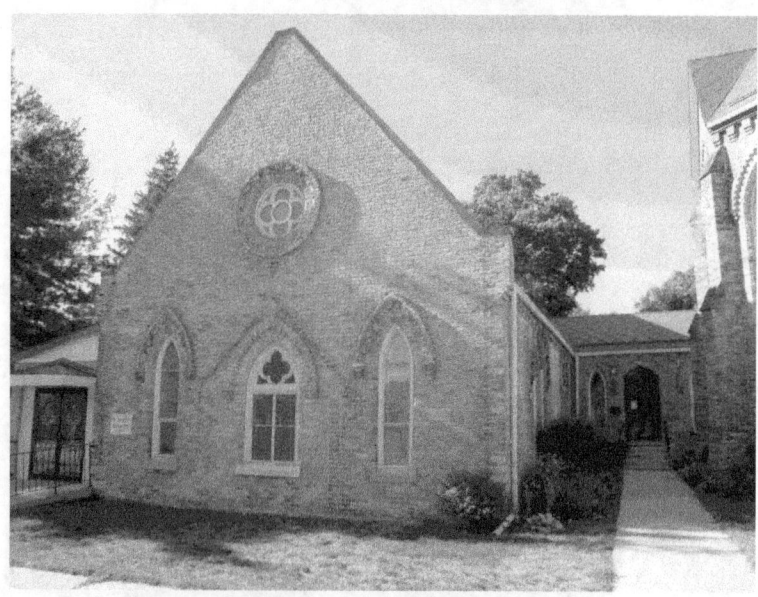

St. George's Parish Hall

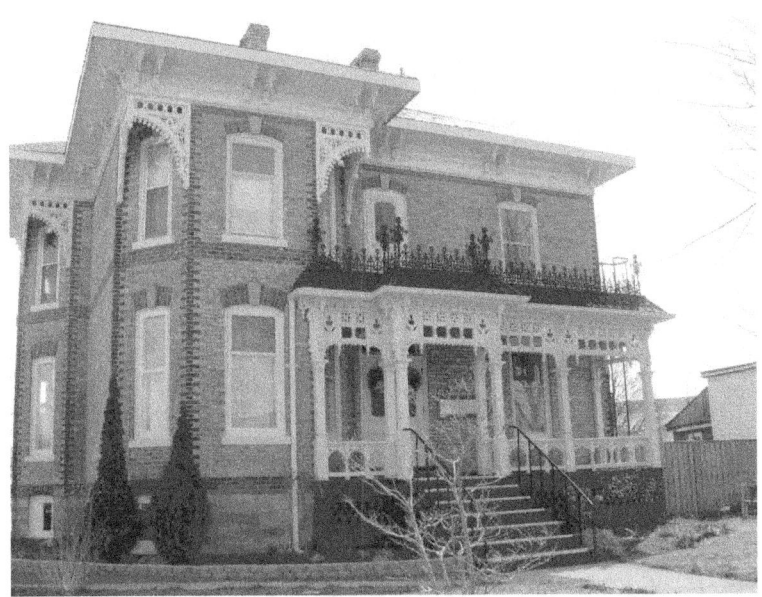

Thyme on 21, 80 Hamilton Street, is a restaurant in a Victorian heritage house built in the late 1870s with iron cresting on the porch and roof peak; scrollwork on the bay window and porch is unique to this community

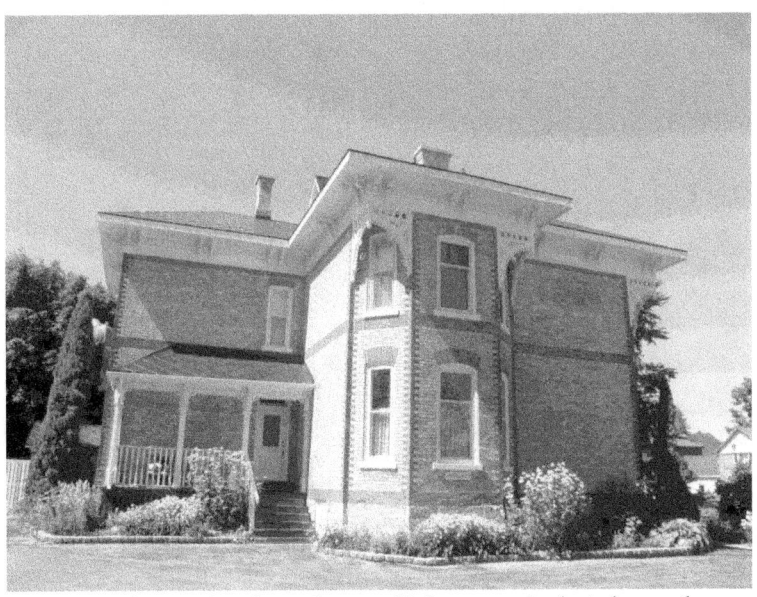

Paired cornice brackets, dichromatic brickwork, local yellow brick

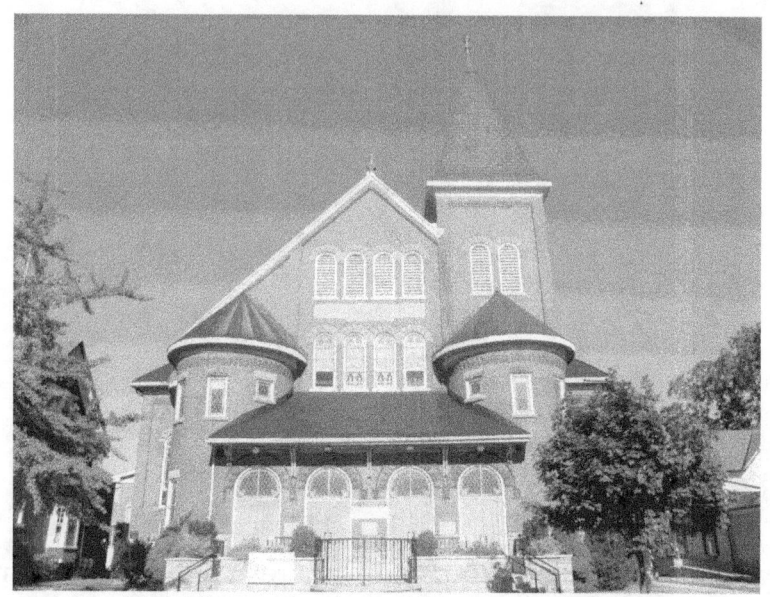

North's Methodist Church – A.D. 1905
Now Trinity United Church

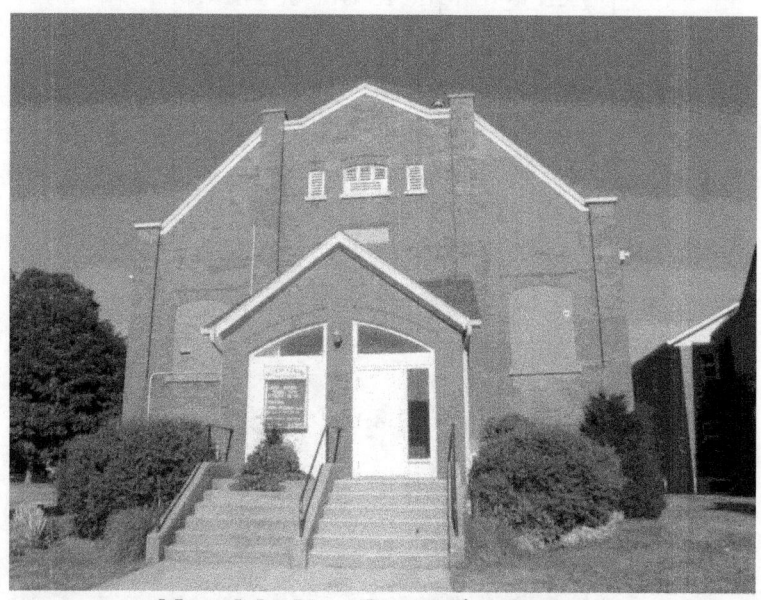

Now MacKay Centre for Seniors

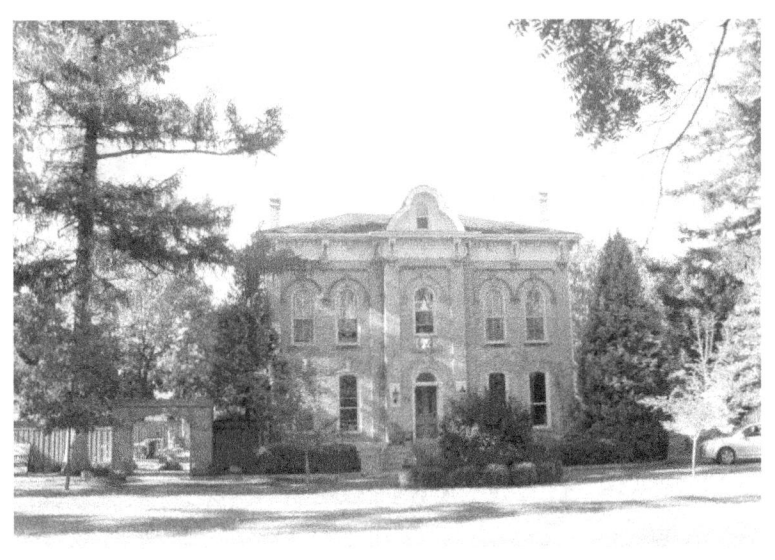

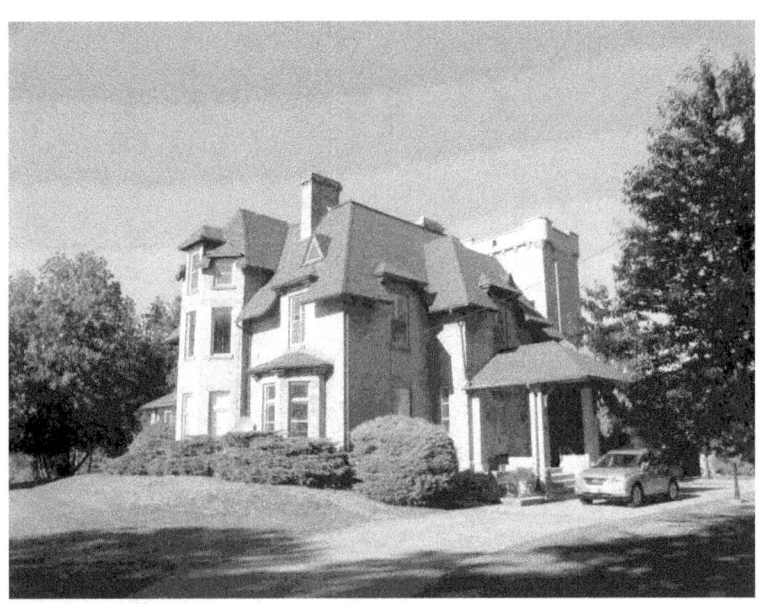

#92

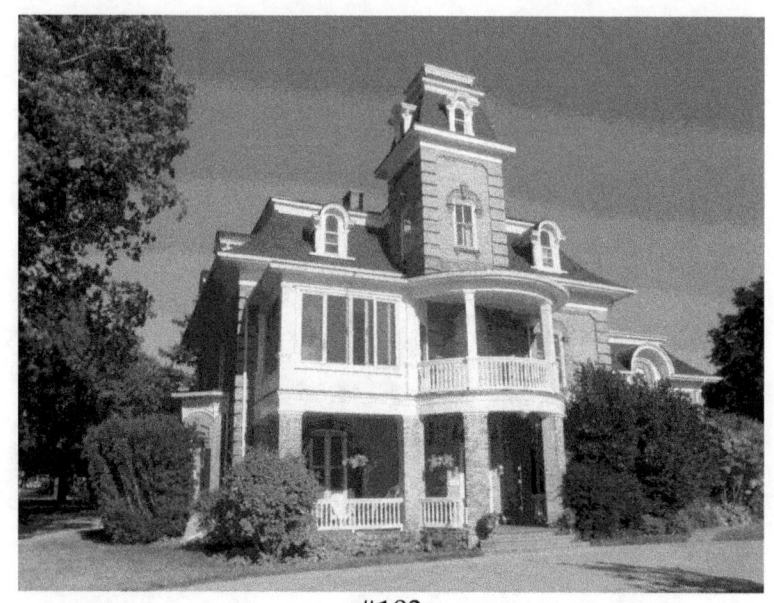

#103

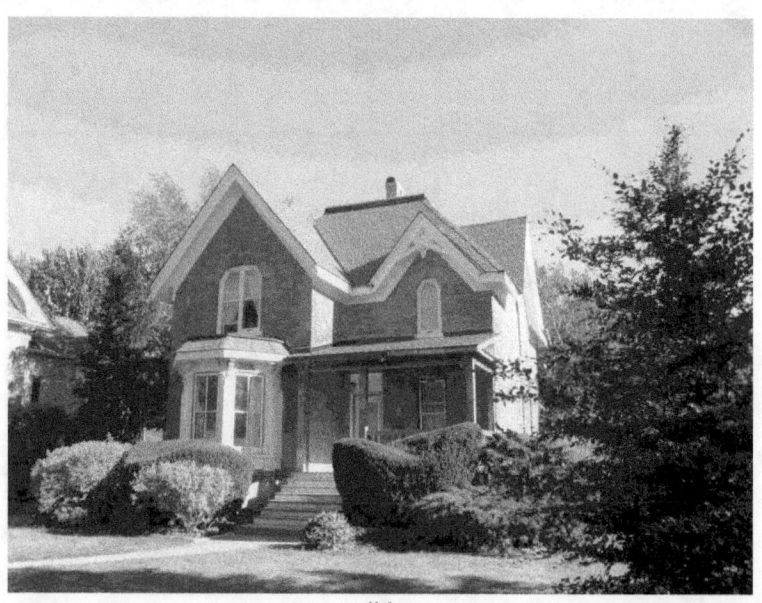

#1

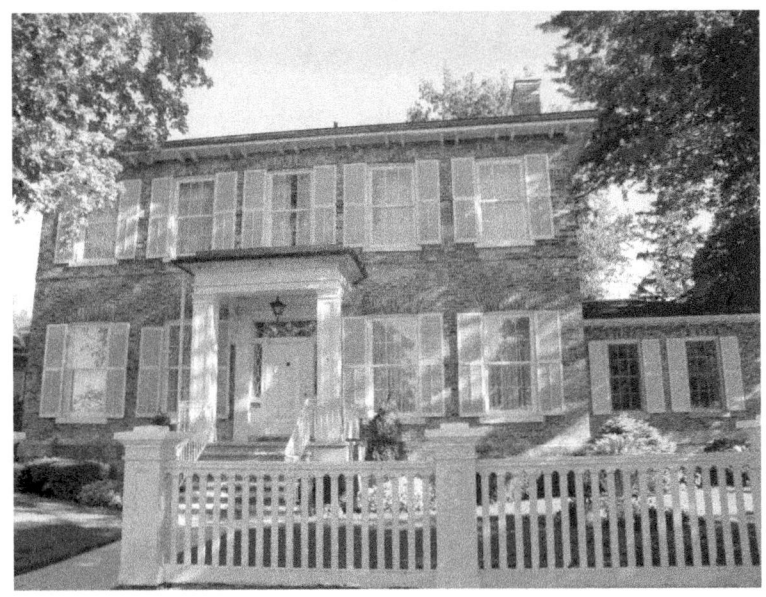

#5

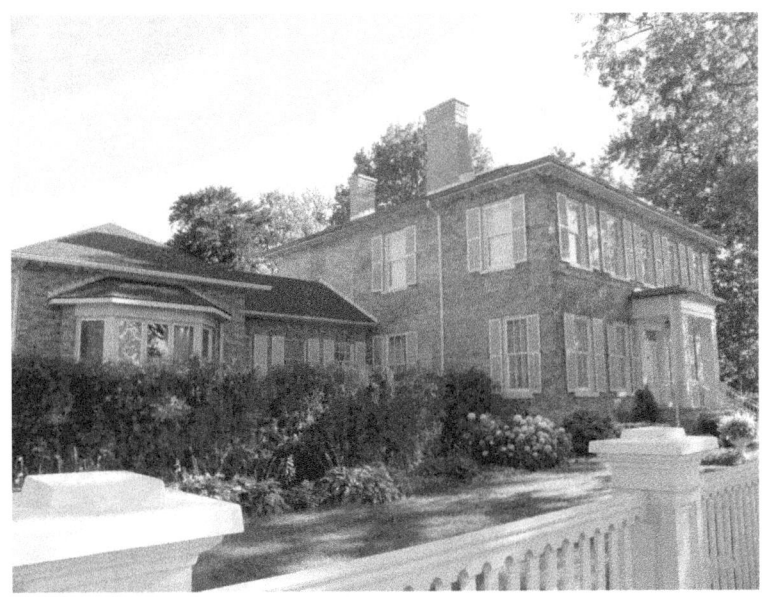

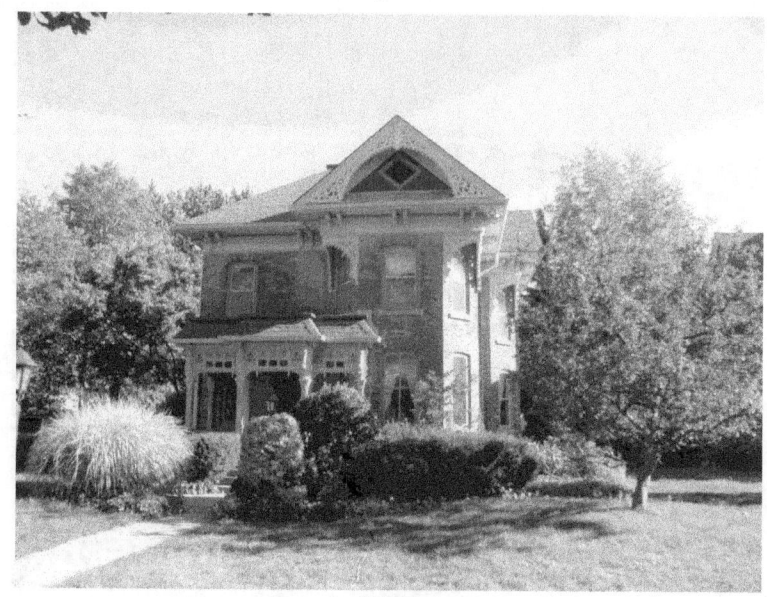

#181

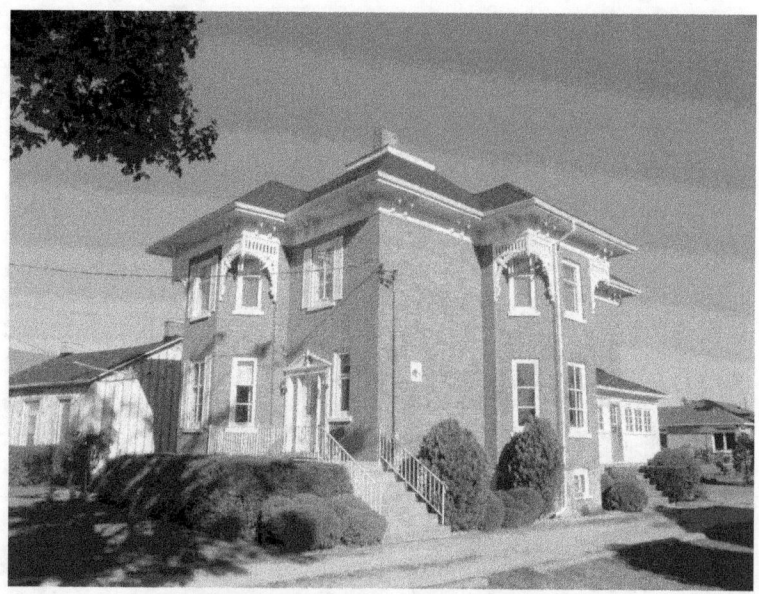

Red brick, paired cornice brackets,
Fancy trim around upper windows

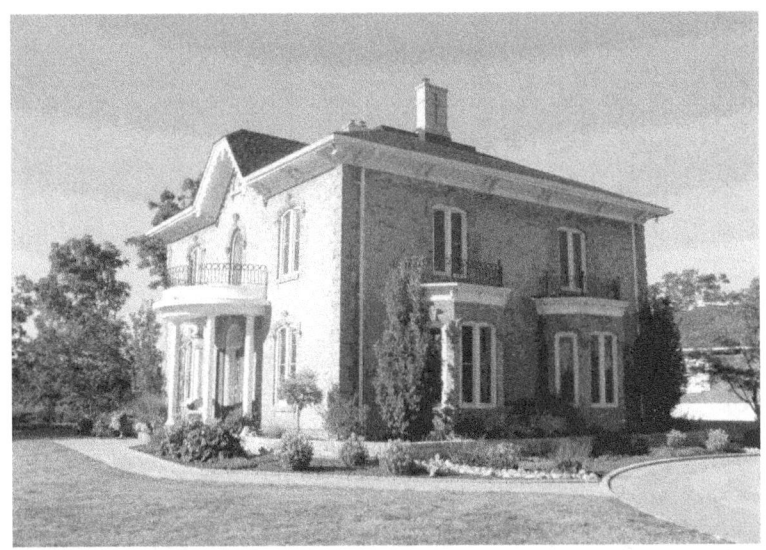

Iron cresting above front entrance and above bay windows,
paired cornice brackets under eaves

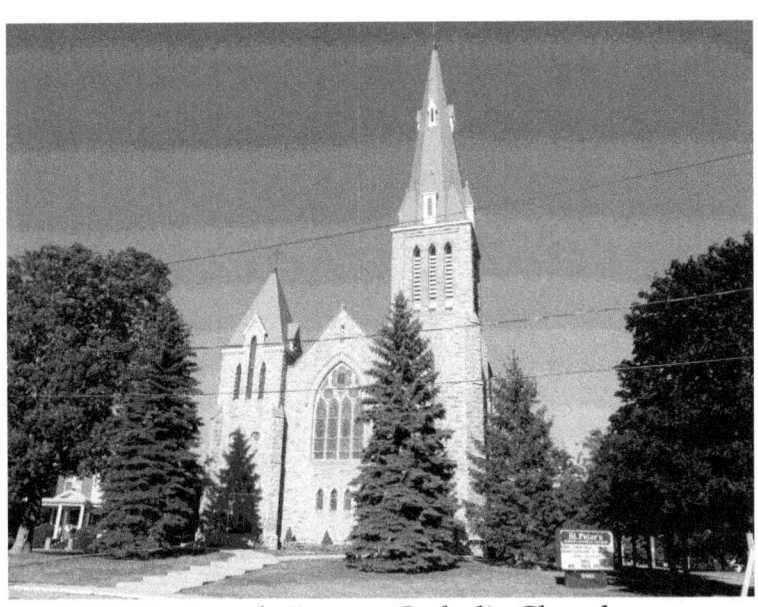

St. Peter's Roman Catholic Church
150 North Street

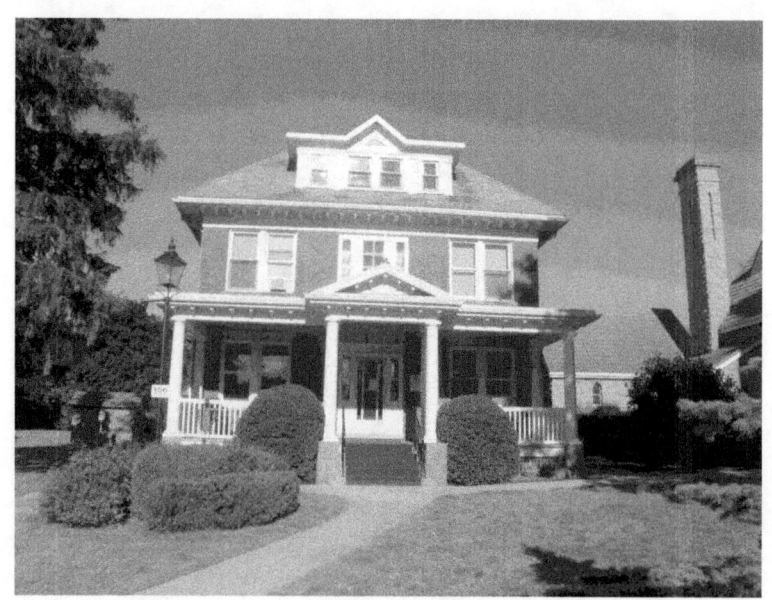

156 North Street

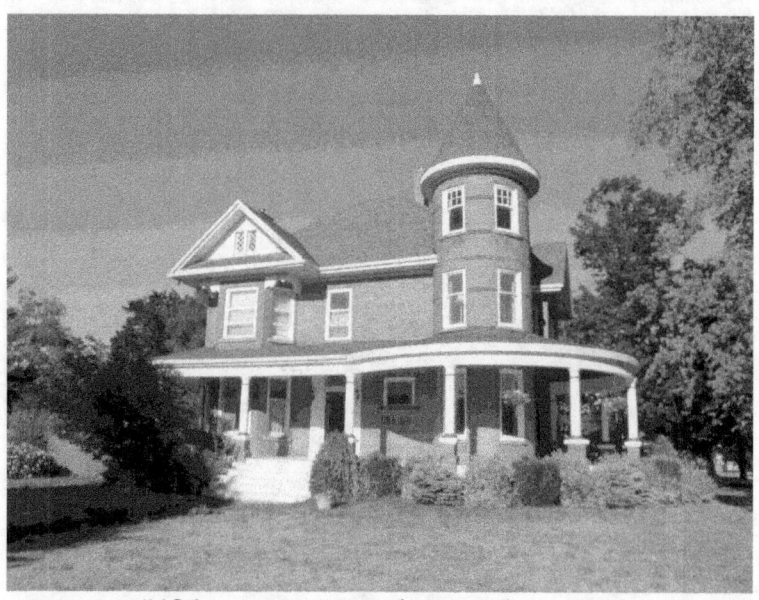

#126 – wraparound veranda, turret

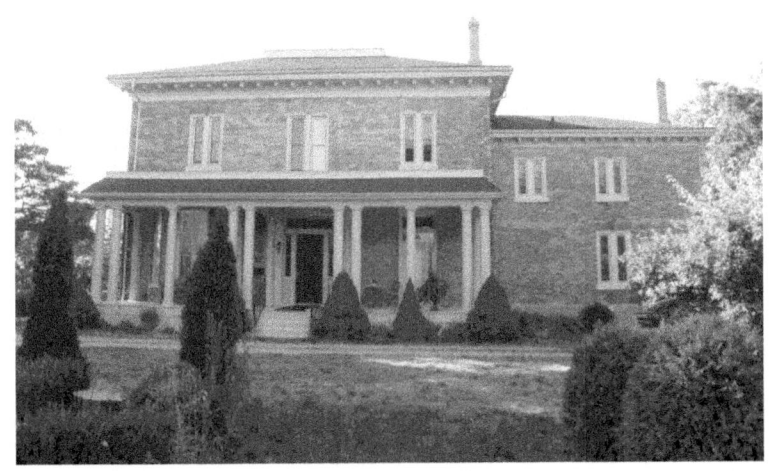

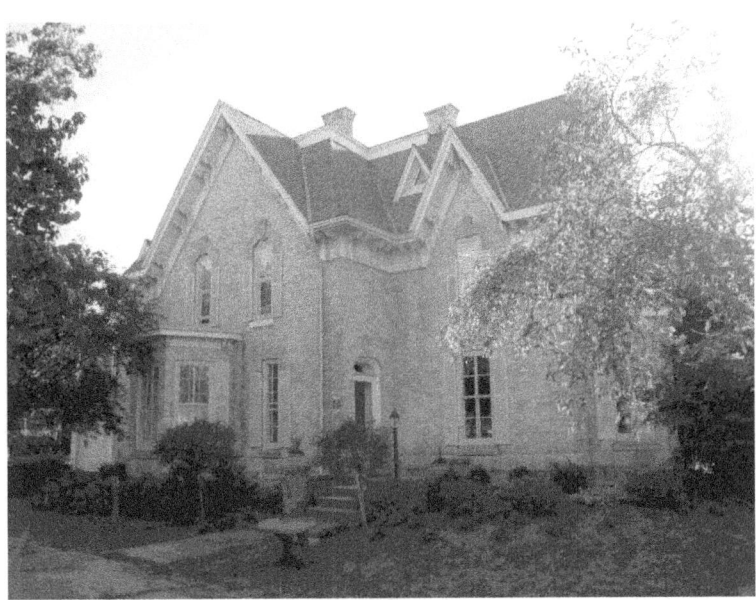

16 – cornice brackets, Gothic-style arches

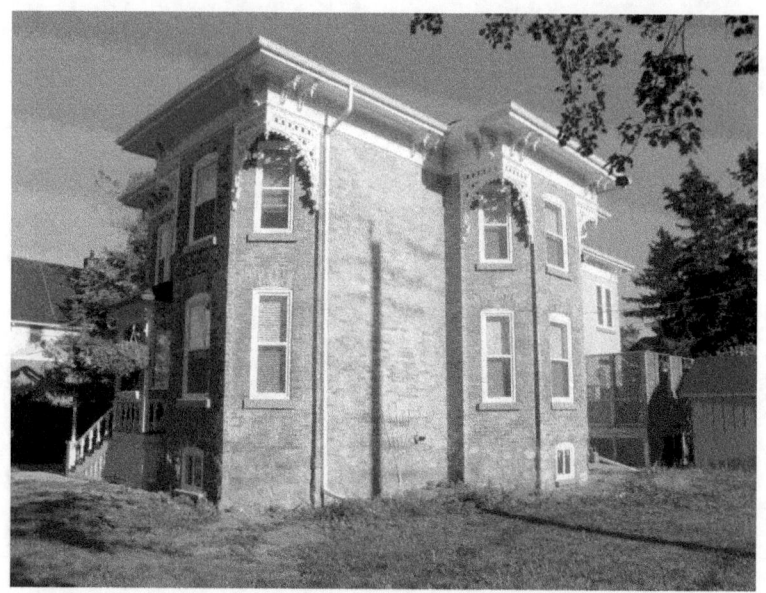

Paired cornice brackets, fancy trim above windows

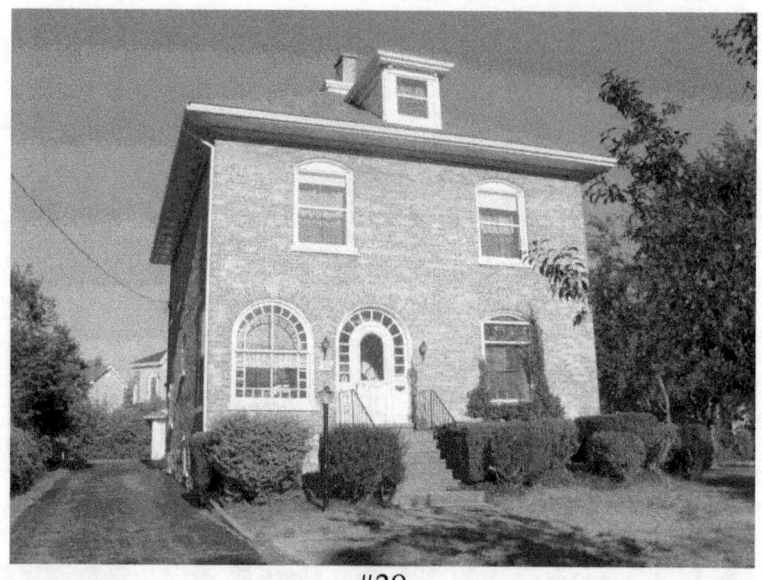

#39

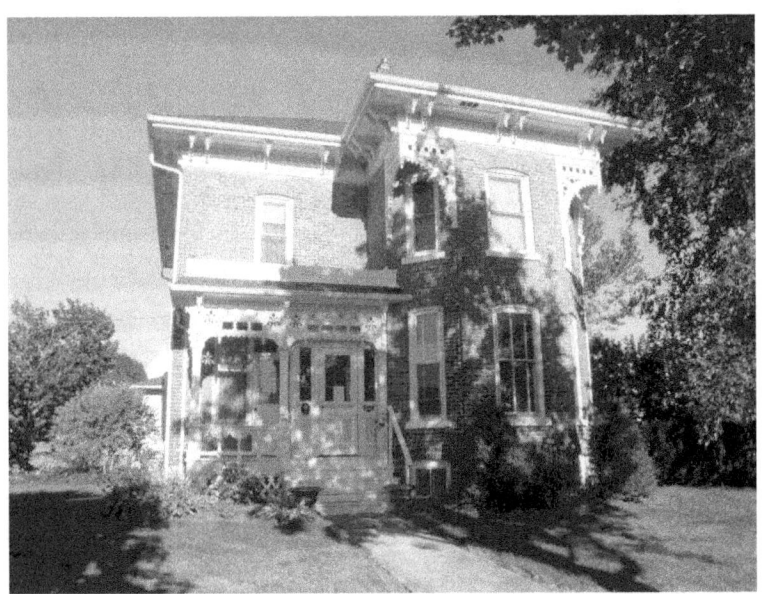

Red brick, fancy trim on porch and upper windows

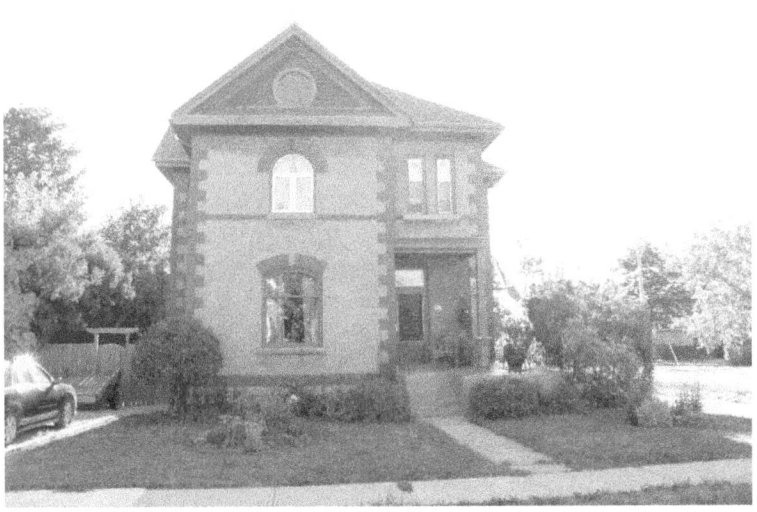

#32 – dichromatic brickwork (2 colours)

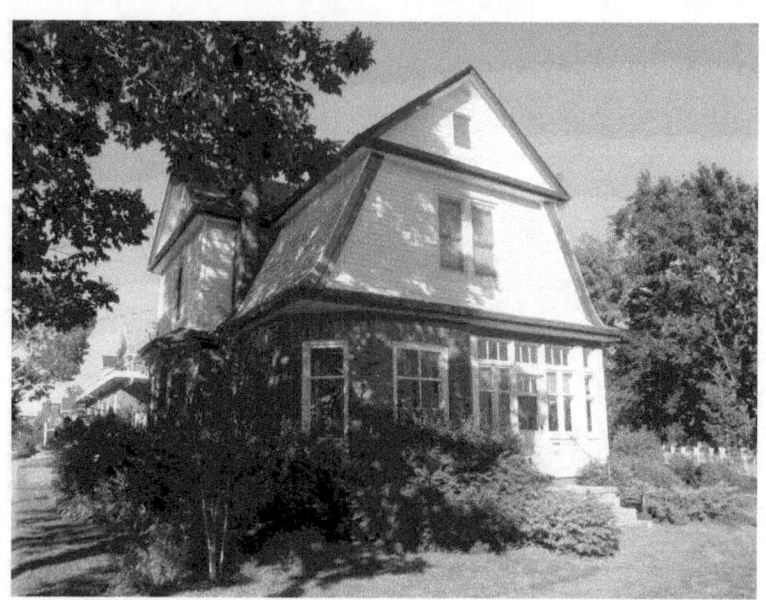

Red brick on lower level, unique shape

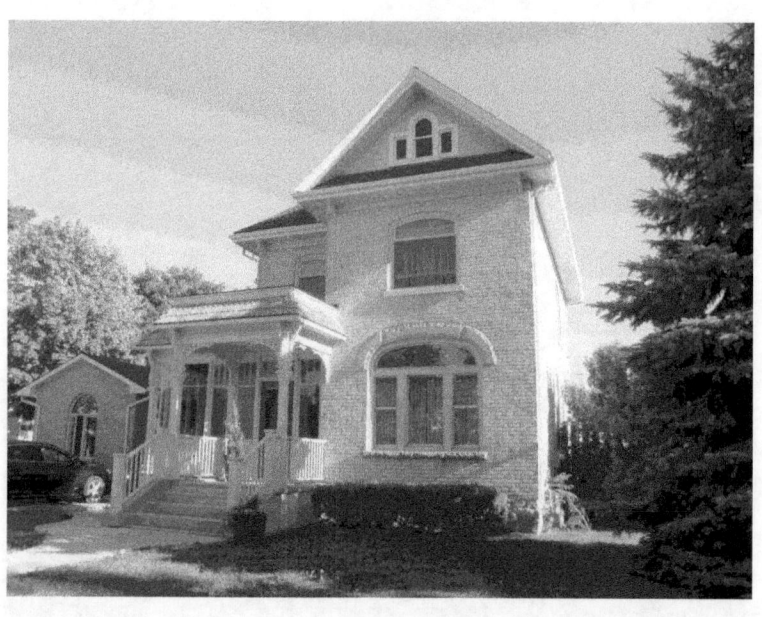

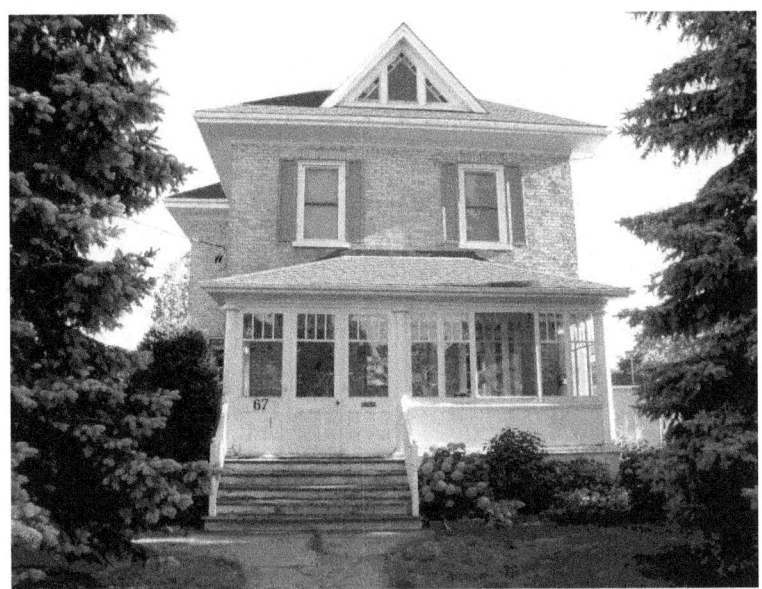

#67

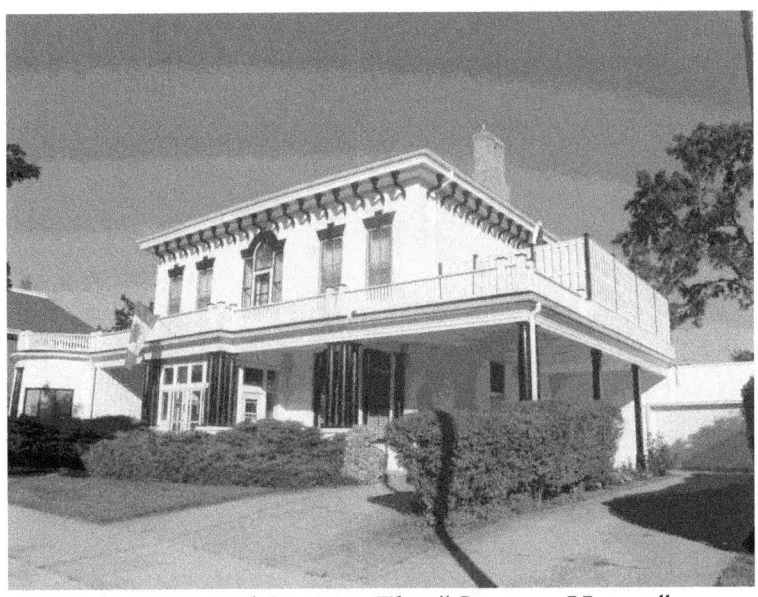

65 Montreal Street – The "Garrow House"
Georgian style with large front windows and two end
chimneys, Palladian window, decorative brackets

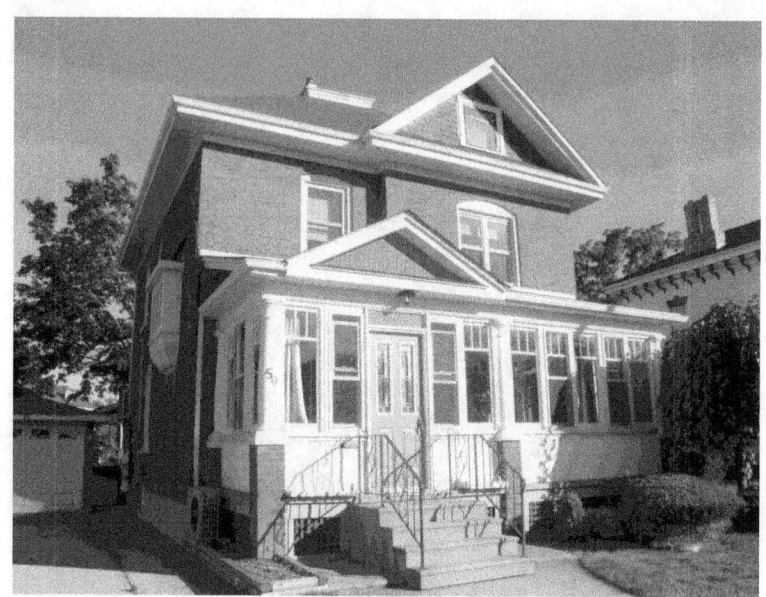

#59

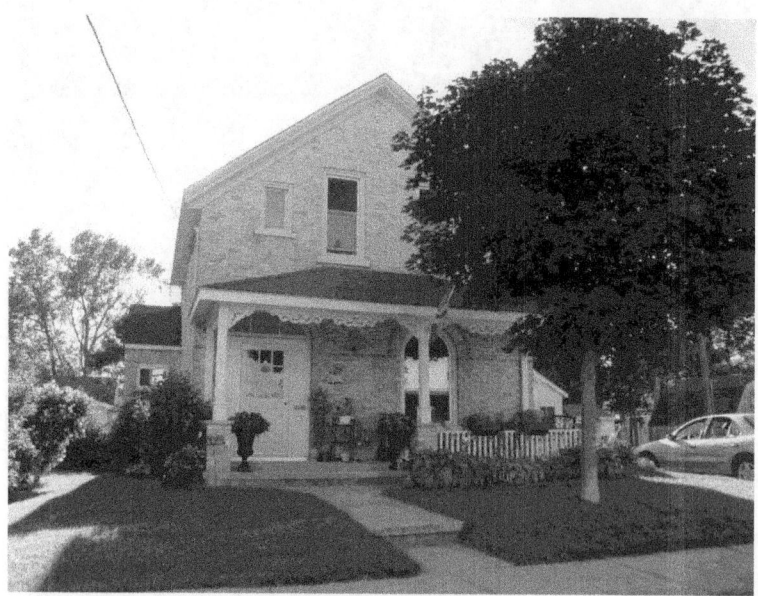

1 Maitland Road

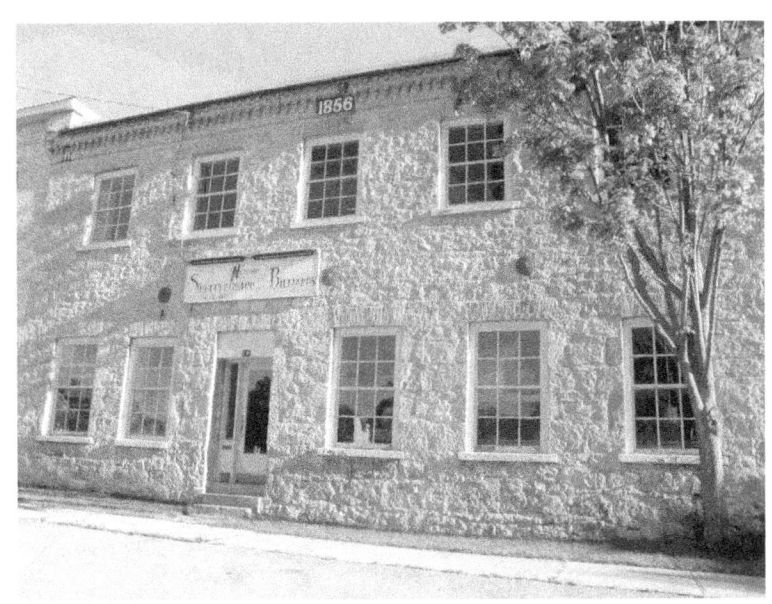

National Shuffleboard and Billiards - 1856

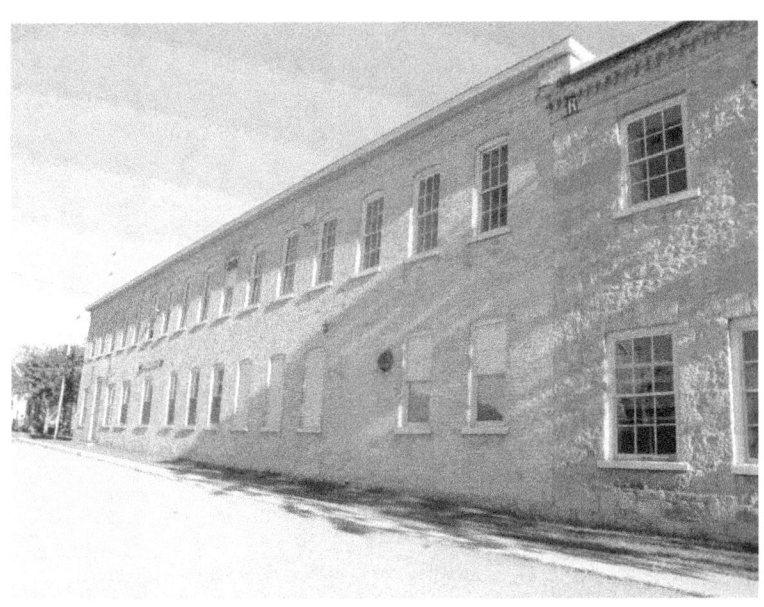

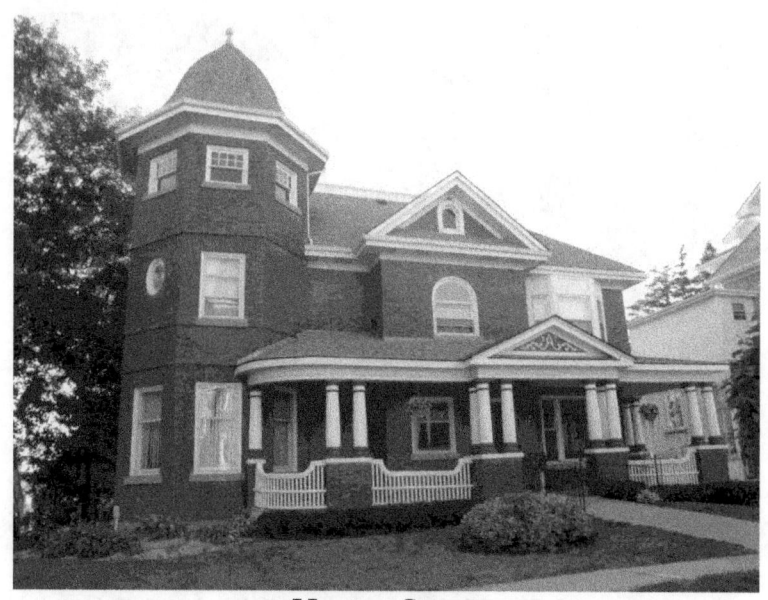

Horton Street

Damage still evident in 2012 after the tornado

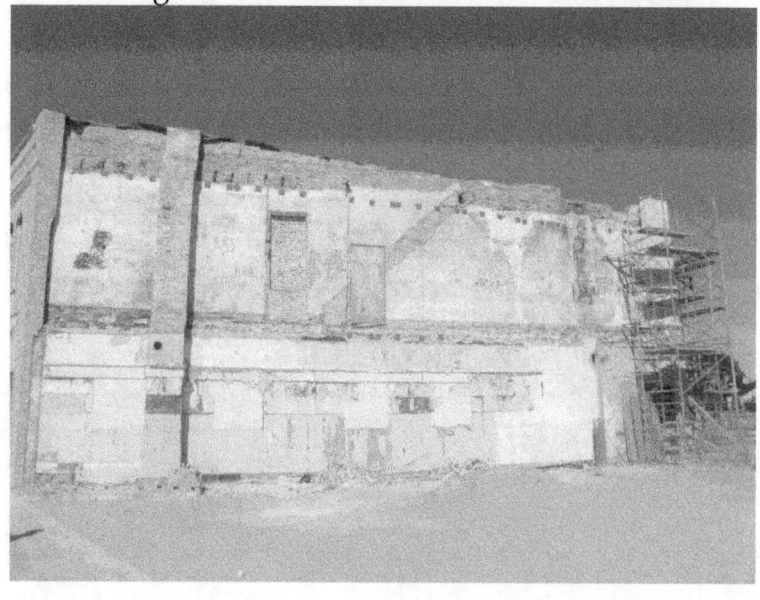